CW00421865

LAW OF ATTRACTION SHORTCUT SECRETS

A powerful approach to reprogram your mind for prosperity with Hypnosis, NLP & Brainwave Entrainment

No 1 In The Cogni-Fusion Mind Expansion Technology Series

Author: Maria McMahon, BSc, Dip. H.E.Hyp/NLP/BSc

Cover Design: Archangel Ink

All images used with permission or under license.

Copyright© - Maria McMahon 2016

Disclaimer

Acknowledgements

No person succeeds alone... we all need help, from family, friends, colleagues, and most of all, source... that higher power that we know looks down on us with love and guides us through the storms...

I am blessed to have a loving family, loyal friends, and a superb support network of heart-centered authors and entrepreneurs.

I would like to thank the following, for all you do, for all your help, for your inspiration to me and to the world. I love you all!

My brother and business partner Declan McMahon: I'm so proud of you for taking a huge leap of faith into the unknown with me.

Else Byskov: the most inspiring author I have ever read, and who I now have the pleasure of calling a dear friend.

Steven Aitchison: for making the world a better place, and taking as many people along with you as you possibly can. You've taught so many people that one can make a difference... and as a result, that one has become thousands.

My Mastermind Group: you know who you are, and your support over these past months has made a world of difference in my life. You guys rock!

My YDF/FB Friends: you are all so inspiring and I'm delighted to be part of your lives and your journeys.

My affiliates: your support over the past few years has been fantastic. I'm particularly indebted to my Singaporean and Malaysian friends... you are always a joy to work with and I can't thank you enough.

We are never alone... reach out and you too will see... the world is full of wonderful people!

TESTIMONIALS

Praise for Law of Attraction Shortcut Secrets

"I have read many books on the law of attraction, going back to the New Thought Movement of the early 1900s that included such authors as Haanel, Hill, Atkinson, Allen and the like on up to the present day. Included among the many techniques I have tried were various brain entrainment and self-hypnotic methods. So, I have long realized that we create our own reality and have been consciously manifesting mine for quite a bit of time now. Being introduced to Law of Attraction Shortcut Secrets System, and learning and understanding the concepts underlying it was like preaching to the choir.

For the system to "work", something out of the ordinary would need to take place to convince me that it, apart from my normal daily intentions, was providing neural re-patterning over and above what was already taking place and that events would need to manifest to demonstrate its effectiveness.

Right away I knew after a few days that this was a powerful neural reprogramming and visualization system. I instantly became entranced with it. The relaxation and peacefulness I experienced was extraordinary indeed. But the real proof is in the pudding as they say. Shortly after the first month, and within a few days of starting the part which deals with Gratitude, I received word that a rather large project, which had been on hold, if you can believe it, for 15 years, was no longer on hold and that I was to get started upon it right away. Needless to say I was blown away. As I said earlier, I don't believe in coincidences or accidents or chance. We create our reality, and the timing of this project with the onset of using the LoA SS System was, in my mind, synchronistic manifestation to the highest degree. The System takes into account the possibility that people may not initially believe that they are manifesting their reality; it matters not. Trying it is the first step to manifestation, and so very much worth it.

What a process you have here Maria… it's superb! Several months later, we have projects coming out of our ears!"

Dennis Grega, Ph.D

Co-creator of the following sites:

AfterlifeData.com

VoicesAcrossTheVeil.com

AfterlifeLibrary.com

"I just wanted to share with you the break-through I have experienced by listening to your first recording. I realized that my belief that I was sick was no longer a fact but self-

sabotage. Being sick no longer serves me so I can choose to let it go. This System has really turned my life around."

Marion Black, Australia

"The videos, books & audios I've looked at before didn't address anything. It was like "change your mindset – listen to these and you'll get a gazillion dollars in 30 days". But they never addressed the mindset BEHIND the issues. Law of Attraction Shortcut Secrets is straightforward and walks you through how to discover your blockages and allows you to work on those. My mind-set kept getting more and more positive!"

Sandie Longs, Texas

"So last night I listened to the first of your recordings. I managed to release two self-limiting beliefs. One of them was as big as a house. This System really is powerful!"

David Storie, Dubai

"I am a visual person and I dislike audio except as background. However, with your recordings, I was amazed. I have listened to other audios before, but yours are truly unique. Your multi-layering process is incredible and delivers superb results. My body and conscious mind felt relaxed but I could feel my subconscious working to assimilate all the *material at the subliminal level. I have never experienced anything like it - absolutely fantastic."*

Perry Jones , Massachusetts

Contents

Introduction 15

CHAPTER 1 19

MP3 Downloads Instructions 19

How To Get Your MP3s / 'Law of Attraction Shortcut Secrets' System Downloads 20

Discover Why the 'Law of Attraction Shortcut Secrets' System Is Going to Change Your Mind-set Forever 21

What This System Will Do for You and Why It Will Work Where Others Have Failed 23

How Do I Know This System Works? 7 Irrefutable Reasons 26

The 7 Key Issues People Struggle with in Making the Law of Attraction Work 27

Bonuses Galore 28

The Psychology, Brain Science and Terminology behind Cogni-Fusion . 29

What is Cogni-Fusion? 29

Basic Brain Science – fMRIs and EEGs 32

Neuroplasticity 32

Brainwave Entrainment (BWE) 34

Binaural Beats 34

Isochronic Tones 35

The benefits of using BWE with Binaural Beats/Isochronic Tones: 36

Understanding Brainwaves: Alpha/Beta/Delta/Theta/Gamma 38

Subliminal Messages 41

"Kaser, V.A. "The Effects of an Auditory Subliminal Perception Message Upon the Production of Images and Dreams". Journal of Nervous and Mental Disease." 42

Another article in Time Magazine in September 1979 entitled: 'Secret Voices: Messages that manipulate" reported: 43

My Belief About Subliminal Messages 44

Your Conscious Mind – Left Brain 46

Your Subconscious mind – Right Brain..46

Why Is My Subconscious Mind So Important In All This? 47

Understanding Repetition...49

Hypnosis..49

Hypnotic Induction 50

Post-hypnotic Suggestion 51

Neuro Linguistic Programming (NLP)..51

Creative Visualization...53

Positive Affirmations..54

Relaxation Techniques 56

Meditation 56

CHAPTER 2 59

Shortcut Secrets: The 7 Critical Blocks to Your Law of Attraction Success:
....59

Key Block No. 1 - Self-limiting Beliefs...60

Self-limiting Beliefs: what are they? 60

How do I identify my self-limiting Beliefs?...65

What areas of your life do you really want/need/desire to change? 71

Realize and accept that you own your self-limiting beliefs 77

Self-limiting Beliefs: my advice 77

Self-limiting Beliefs: my steepest learning curve 78

Key Block No 2: Self Sabotage / Inner Saboteur 79

Eliminating Self Limiting Beliefs & Silencing your Inner Saboteur 80

Self-sabotage/inner saboteur: my advice 80

Self-sabotage/inner saboteur: my steepest learning curve.................81

Key Block No 3: Diamonds from Dust: Unrealistic Expectations...........81

Diamonds from dust: my advice 84

Diamonds from dust: my steepest learning curve 84

Key Block No 4: Shiny Object Syndrome 86

Shiny object syndrome: my advice 87

Shiny object syndrome: my steepest learning curve 87

Key Block No 5: Lack of Patience 88

Lack of patience: my advice 88

Lack of patience: my steepest learning curve...............................89

Key Block No 6: Blame Culture...89

Blame culture: my advice- don't play the blame game 91

Blame culture: my steepest learning curve 92

Key Block No 7: Not Committing to Your Personal Success.................92

Committing to your personal success: my advice..............................93

Committing to your personal success: my steepest learning curve 94

CHAPTER 3 94

Fundamentals of the Universal Laws 94

Understanding the Law of Gratitude 95

Some Famous Quotes from the Super-Wealthy 99

Why The Power Of Emotion Matters To Gratitude 100

Understanding the Law of Attraction 102

The Power of Intention and The Law of Attraction 105

Understanding the Law of Abundance 107

Wealth – An Alternative Definition..113

The 6 Fundamental Steps to Your Success: Shortcut Secrets 114

Can you feel good instantly? How to change Your Vibrational Resonance
....116

Technique No. 1: Using memory based affirmative cues 116

Technique No. 2: Using activity based affirmative cues 118

Technique No. 3: Negativity analysis 119

Some final thoughts 121

Who am I and why should you listen to me?......................................123

Get in Touch with me… 127

CHAPTER 4 130

How to Use The Law of Attraction Shortcut Secrets Cogni-Fusion Mind Expansion Technology MP3s..130

How to use this System..131

Preparation for Listening To The Recordings.........................132

Breakdown of the Law of Attraction Shortcut Secrets Cogni-Fusion Mind Expansion Technology System 137

MP3 1: Blast Your Self-limiting Beliefs 138

MP3 2: Understanding the Law of Gratitude 139

MP3 3: Understanding the Law of Attraction 140

MP3 4: Understanding the Law of Abundance 142

MP3 5: Committing to Your Wealth Creation 143

Bonus MP3 1: Powerhouse 5 - Specifically for daytime listening 144

Bonus MP3 2: Creative Visualization - Nature Trail 144

Bonus MP3 3: Meditation 145

About the Author..147

Final Word From Maria 149

Introduction

Have you tried the Law of Attraction with little success and wondered why you couldn't make it work for you? Have you read dozens of books that sounded amazing when you read them but for some reason, they got relegated to your bookshelf, where they are still gathering dust, or they got lost somewhere on your reading device?

Are you really fed-up with all the big promises that simply didn't deliver? And do you want to really understand why you have failed to make the Law of Attraction work to bring all those powerful but empty promises to life for you?

Do you want to truly understand what is preventing you from having the happiness, success and abundance you desire? And more importantly, do you want a system, not just a mere book, that can help you finally break through the limiting beliefs that are holding you back?

Do you want a system that you can easily implement and that really works? If you are nodding your head now and thinking…. 'Hmmm… I've heard it all before…' I understand. I really do. Because I had heard it all before too. And like you, I was disillusioned and fed-up with all the empty promises.

Yet somehow, deep down, I knew there had to be a way… there had to be truth in everything that had been written about the Law of Attraction, but what was the elusive solution to actually making it work?

In this book, I'm going to share that elusive solution with you, and clearly identify the real reasons why all your previous efforts have failed, and I'm going to give you the tools – real tools – that will enable you to completely reprogram both your conscious and much more importantly, your subconscious mind, to blast all the limiting beliefs into oblivion and clear a path in your brain that will lead you into a whole new way of thinking. Success really can be yours if you follow this system.

But who am I and why should you believe me? Well, I share a bit more of my story later on in the book, but, as a Certified Clinical NLP/Hypnotherapist, BSc. (Psychology), Master Life Coach, Master Law of Attraction Practitioner, Personal Development Author, and lifelong passionate student of making life better by learning, studying and implementing every strategy you care to name, I created a system that blew everything else out of the water. A system that enabled me to effortlessly lose 20lbs after trying for more than 25 years. A system that enabled me to cure my insomnia in two weeks. A system that gave me the courage to leave a 6-figure corporate salary behind to pursue my dream of sharing it with others. And a system that has indeed helped countless people make incredible changes in their lives… the way I did in mine, and the way you can in yours.

If you want to get clear in your mind about why you think the way you do, and how to change that consciously and subconsciously, so that you can have the success, love, joy and happiness that you are seeking, this book, and the accompanying ground-breaking 'Cogni-Fusion' audio training

MP3s that come with it, will show you exactly how it can be done.

Marion Black was one of the first people to try this system and she shared an incredible breakthrough with me. She was holding on to a limiting belief that she was sick... this system helped her dig deep inside, to find the answers that were holding her back, and she was able to let go of that belief... just like that, after holding on to it for years, and move towards a whole new way of thinking and as a result, her life really changed. You too can experience your own breakthrough, and this system will give you the tools and show you exactly how!

I promise that if you follow this system and listen to the recordings that have been specially created to accompany you on your journey to prosperity, within a very short time you will begin to experience a seismic shift in your thinking, just as I, and many of my loyal readers, already have. You will be one of the people who finally 'gets it' and begins to understand the power you have within your self to shape the world according to your desires.

If you want to be one of those people who shapes their world by understanding how their minds work, and how to use scientifically proven technology to make huge leaps forward in getting what they want from life, then this get this book – this system – today. Don't be that person who sits on the fence, waiting for things to happen... be the person who grabs life with both hands and makes it happen!

If you want to learn the secret to shattering self-limiting beliefs, to harnessing the power of the Universal Laws of Attraction, Gratitude and Abundance, to overcome 'Shiny Object Syndrome' and to crush the 7 Critical Blocks that are getting in the way of your Law of Attraction Success – with an absolutely unique and ground-breaking system... then go right now to the buy button and claim your copy today. A new world of joy, abundance and prosperity is waiting for you!

CHAPTER 1

Welcome to Law of Attraction Shortcut Secrets: A powerful approach to reprogram your mind for prosperity with Hypnosis, NLP & Brainwave Entrainment

MP3 Downloads Instructions

Firstly, welcome and thank you for purchasing this System. As you have already seen from the book description, Law of Attraction Shortcut Secrets is much more than just a book. Although it is packed with valuable information to help you build the foundation for Changing Your World From The Inside Out, the real power is in the unique set of Cogni-Fusion MP3s that I created to work in harmony with this book. So please DO NOT overlook this vital next step. The 'Shortcut Secrets' lie in the power of these ground-breaking MP3s, which are unlike any you will have heard before. Later in this book, I will explain all about Cogni-Fusion and how I came to create this unique type of therapeutic recording.

How To Get Your MP3s / 'Law of Attraction Shortcut Secrets' System Downloads

So, first things first. Please click the link below to go to the Private Membership Registration site.

http://www.mariamcmahon.com/membership-signup

When it opens, enter your personal log in details. Once you do that, you will need to go to your inbox to confirm your subscription. This is a password protected membership site and you will be issued with login details so that you can access the site any time. You will get immediate access, with simple instructions to download all the 5 Core Cogni-Fusion MP3s and the 3 Bonus MP3s that comes with this System – and some Surprise Bonuses too.

If you have any problems whatsoever, please email support@cogni-fusion.com and we'll get right back to you. Once you have done that, save everything is a safe place, as you will need to easily access all of them once you have read the book.

On that note, please let me point out something very important. You may be tempted to just go straight to the MP3s and start listening to them. Please DO NOT do this! You really need to understand the psychology behind how they were created and how this relates to helping you change your mind-set – consciously and subconsciously, but if you skip the vital reading of this book, you will miss out on really important concepts. I do not want you to jeopardize or sabotage your own success before you even start! So please, read this book first if you want to get the very best out of this System.

Discover Why the 'Law of Attraction Shortcut Secrets' System Is Going to Change Your Mind-set Forever

Congratulations and welcome to the start of your 'Law of Attraction Shortcut Secrets' journey. The fact you have chosen this System reveals to me you want to massively change your mind-set to make the law of attraction work for you, tackle the things in your life that are not working, and start living life on your own fresh new terms! This book, along with the accompanying set of 5 MP3s, and 3 bonus MP3s, will give you the incredible jump-start you need to start changing your world from the inside out; something that I know every one of us has the innate power to do. My System will provide you with a proven, fast, effective introduction to the fundamental Universal Laws of Gratitude, Attraction and Abundance and show you how understanding these laws can change your life very quickly, enabling you to:

- Gain immediate confidence in your ability to succeed in anything you do
- Eliminate all doubts and fears about taking control of your life
- Change the pattern of negative thinking that has stopped you from achieving the life you truly deserve
- Begin attracting the abundance you deserve, whether that is in the area of love, money, health, self-esteem, or all of them.

… and much more.

People today are busier than ever. You have so much to cram into your life already. This is why I wanted to create a System that could be digested in a short book. This is followed up with 5 results-oriented MP3 Cogni-Fusion recordings that have proven highly beneficial for me and countless others who have listened to them.

This System is therefore one of the simplest ever designed. I wanted to keep it as short as possible whilst driving home the key points in a way that would be fast, fun and effective. You will not be bogged down with lengthy theoretical concepts or complex psychology. I have presented the information here in a simple format anyone can understand and work with. I have designed this System with the complete beginner or 'newbie' to the Laws of the Universe in mind. However, even if you already have extensive knowledge of the Law of Attraction, you will still find something new in here in the form of my breakthrough MP3 Cogni-Fusion recordings. They are an innovative new mechanism for delivering these truths to your subconscious mind.

To get the absolute best from my system you will need to get a notebook or journal. Once you have read this book, you'll see why. But I'm not going to insist you follow a schedule of writing every day. I'm going to suggest that you decide when you need to write things down, and then you'll do it. Because you are the one in control of your success, I am not. My

System will however, show you quickest, fastest, easiest way to get the results you truly desire and deserve.

What This System Will Do for You and Why It Will Work Where Others Have Failed

Age-old wisdom, new technology

I have read hundreds of books on the Laws of the Universe over the past 25 years. What I realized during my research is that most of them are saying basically the same things. One of the most critical of these is the concept of energy; everything is made up of energy vibrating at different frequencies. We are all energy. This has been verified in quantum physics. And our thoughts are energy. What we think can be measured in brainwaves. This is scientific fact. What I am doing here is not revealing anything new if you are already familiar with these amazing laws. If you are not familiar with them, rest assured they are real and this book will convince you of that. They work. Thousands of writers who have written books about them know this and I know it, because they have worked for me.

So firstly, this book will give you a super-quick, comprehensive course in understanding the basic terminology in a quick and easy format. If you have never heard of such terms as Hypnotherapy, Brainwave Entrainment, NLP, Law of Attraction, Law of Abundance, and the power of your subconscious, then by the time you finish reading this book you will have all the knowledge and tools you need to become a proficient practitioner of the Universal Law of Attraction. If you have heard of them but have not had a great deal of success this System will change all that. You will be able to create success if you just follow the System.

Secondly, what makes this System so incredibly different, and incredibly effective is my breakthrough formula. It is the way I have combined modern technology to create a brand new protocol, Cogni-Fusion Mind Expansion Technology, that brings together a powerful blend of Brainwave Entrainment, Hypnotherapy, NLP, Subliminal Messages, music and the sounds of nature to create a unique new approach to mind programming. Bear in mind that sound vibration is also energy; when you hear, your brain/ears are responding to energy frequencies. Therefore, my Cogni-Fusion compilations are giving your conscious and subconscious minds vibrational energy, in a way you have not encountered before.

This is where the real power of this System begins, with over 7 hours of breakthrough MP3 Cogni-Fusion/Brainwave Entrainment recordings that will change your life. These recordings will suffuse both your conscious and subconscious minds with a deep understanding of the universal concepts we'll discuss in this System. What's more, you will be blown away when you hear the complex six to eight layer Cogni-Fusion MP3s and realize just how much positive subconscious reprogramming they contain.

My key objective in writing this book and preparing the accompanying MP3 System was to keep it as simple as possible, as I have already mentioned. I could write hundreds of pages on the subject, (and I do plan to write several more books in the Cogni-Fusion Personal Development Series) but this System is designed with the complete 'newbie' in mind. It need not be complicated. Once you grasp the fundamentals from this System, you will have a solid foundation on which to build your knowledge as you too become fascinated with the Laws of the Universe. This System is a complete package that will enable you to re-program your subconscious mind, save you years of hard work, and see results fast.

My subliminal and Cogni-Fusion System works so well that you will see amazing results in your life. You will feel more optimistic and confident than you have ever felt before.

How Do I Know This System Works? 7 Irrefutable Reasons

The information in this book is presented in a concise, easy to understand format, giving you the most important information you need to understand this System and make it work for you. It should only take you a couple of hours to read this book.

The Cogni-Fusion (Brainwave Entrainment, Hypnotherapy, NLP and Subliminal Programming) MP3s I have created are unique and simply life changing. With absolutely no effort on your part other than the time it takes to listen to them.

Furthermore, I have designed this stunning System to eliminate the 7 key obstacles holding you back from success.

The 7 Key Issues People Struggle with in Making the Law of Attraction Work

1. **Self-Limiting Beliefs**
2. **Self-Sabotage**
3. **Expecting Diamonds from Dust: Unrealistic Expectations**
4. **'Shiny Object Syndrome'**
5. **Lack of Patience**
6. **Blame Culture**
7. **Not Committing to Your Success**

I will discuss each of these in greater detail so that you fully understand them and I will outline which MP3 recording to use to overcome each particular block. It is critical to understand these 7 issues from both a realistic conscious perspective and from a 'subconscious mind-set' perspective. They are the most important components of making the Law of Attraction work. Once you get your head around these issues and start regularly listening to my MP3 recordings, you will be unstoppable! I have created each recording with these issues in mind and they are covered audibly and subliminally. Beyond powerful.

Bonuses Galore

I have also included 3 bonus MP3s containing Brainwave Entrainment, Meditation, Creative Visualization and Subliminal Messages. These will further penetrate your subconscious to help eliminate the 7 key obstacles standing in your way, making this an incredibly powerful subconscious programming Program.

One of these, the 'Law of Attraction Powerhouse Five' is specially designed for daytime listening with Isochronic Tones. This includes ALL of the positive affirmations at a subliminal level so you can play it during your working hours if this is practical. That's almost 7 hours of deep subconscious programming that will accompany you on your journey to achieving incredible success and living the life of your dreams.

I have also constructed five 30-minute versions of the Core 5 MP3s for you to use once you have listened to the full versions. These will reduce the time you need to spend listening to the recordings but will still have the same impact. I recommend you listen to the full versions initially in order to fully 'prime' your mind for success. Once you have done this, shorter listening sessions will still be highly effective.

The benefit is that you are getting over 9 hours of incredibly relaxing and life-changing tools that will turbo-charge your subconscious mind, reprogramming it in a way you never thought possible. You will be stunned at the change in your mind-set and once you start to experience the results, you will not want to stop. You will be hungry for more. This will undoubtedly be the start of your love affair with the power of the universe and the power of your own subconscious mind. It is awesome.

The Psychology, Brain Science and Terminology behind Cogni-Fusion

How are the MP3s recordings made?

Each MP3 recording is carefully designed, layered and mixed until I have the perfect combination for each session. I have teamed up with top Brainwave Entrainment and Hypnotherapy Recording Technology Partners to bring these incredible recordings to life.

Below I want to explain all the different components I researched and how they were integrated to bring Cogni-Fusion Mind Expansion Technology to life.

What is Cogni-Fusion?

Cognition is defined as being "of, relating to, being, or involving conscious intellectual activity (as in thinking, reasoning, or remembering)". Cogni-Fusion is the term I use for my System that takes you away from your cognitive perspective of rational, conscious thinking. It does this by combining Hypnotherapy, NLP and Brainwave Entrainment to create a 'fusion' into your subconscious by means of multi-layered, complex and highly effective MP3 recordings. It is not to be confused with Cognitive Fusion, most commonly associated with Acceptance & Commitment Therapy (ACT) which is a different therapeutic approach altogether.

My Cogni-Fusion recording takes Audio Training for personal change to a whole new level because I build in up to 7 layers, to include relaxation induction in dual audio and including all the therapeutic techniques mentioned above. The great thing about my system is that the Audio Training is targeting different hemispheres of your brain all at the same time.

This does 2 things. Firstly, if you are inclined to be overly analytical or prone to self-sabotage, the multiple layers override your conscious objections to change because while you are listening and thinking about one thing being said, your subconscious has no choice but to absorb the powerful therapeutic messages being fed into it on another level.

Secondly, because I am using specifically selected brainwave entrainment, your brain is literally induced into a deep state of trance – or trance-formation as I like to think of it! And that's when big changes can and WILL happen.

But that's not all there is to this system. To make this Audio Training even more effective, I've spent countless hours experimenting with different audio technology and added in a number of engaging effects so that you are hearing voices sometimes in your left ear, sometimes your right ear, sometimes in the middle of your brain, and sometimes panning across all three. That's one of my personal favorite techniques because it's got a real WOW factor to it when you listen with headphones – it feel like you have three brains!

The benefit of this technique is that it creates rapid, effective change in your behavior by overriding your ability to consciously raise self-sabotaging objections. So no matter how long you have held on to past pains or negative thinking, Cogni-Fusion creates rapid and effective change in your subconscious, by over-riding the negative programming that you want to eliminate but can't.

In essence, Cogni-Fusion enables you to reprogram your (conscious) mind AND rewire your brain (subconscious) for stunning results. If you'd like to watch a short video I made about Cogni-Fusion, please click the link here:

http://maria.rurl.me/whatiscognifusion

Basic Brain Science – fMRIs and EEGs

These are obviously huge areas of scientific study, but I'm going to give you the very briefest details here in case you've never heard of them.

fMRI: Functional magnetic resonance imaging, or fMRI, is a technique for measuring brain activity. It works by detecting the changes in blood oxygenation and flow that occur in response to neural activity. When a brain area is more active it consumes more oxygen and to meet this increased demand blood flow increases to the active area. fMRI can be used to produce maps showing which parts of the brain are involved in a particular mental process.

EEG: an electroencephalogram is a machine used to make images of the brain while it is performing various cognitive tasks. Data are gathered by putting electrodes on the scalp to measure activity and the information can be printed out for study. Both fMRIs and EEGs have been used extensively in Brainwave Entrainment Research.

Neuroplasticity

Neuroplasticity (also known as 'brain plasticity) is an umbrella term that describes the brain changes that occur in response to different experiences. It encompasses both synaptic and non-synaptic plasticity, and refers to changes in neural pathways due to changes in behavior, environment, neural processes, thinking, emotions and changes in the brain resulting from bodily/brain injury.

Simply put, it's how your brain 'reads' or 'decodes' everything that you experience in life. But what is really amazing is that the plasticity aspect refers to your brain's ability to change, to form new pathways and connections; an ability that you have throughout your whole life. There are many different mechanisms of neuroplasticity ranging from the growth of new connections to the creation of new neurons within the brain. Much research has shown that even damaged brains have the ability to heal - something that was thought impossible as recently as 20 years ago.

There is an ever-growing (and very exciting) body of research showing that the mind can influence the brain, altering the long-held scientific belief that the brain controlled or housed the mind. The implications of this new research is way beyond the scope of this book, but they are nonetheless incredibly exciting for me because I believe that this research shows, without doubt, that what we think about literally changes our brain. In addition, meditation has been shown to have a distinct effect on brain activity and brainwave entrainment most certainly changes brainwave states.

I am so attuned to brainwave entrainment now that I can literally feel the shift in my brain as I drift down to the deepest levels of meditation using deep delta brainwave entrainment.

Brainwave Entrainment (BWE)

BWE is the practice of using the technology of Binaural Beats and Isochronic Tone sound waves to cause brainwave frequencies to 'entrain' into a desired state of relaxation, focus, or meditation. BWE most frequently uses Binaural Beats and Isochronic Tones at its core, although there are also visual means of achieving BWE. Research has shown brainwave patterns look markedly different after an entrainment session.

Binaural Beats

Human ears are binaural – basically, we hear with both our ears. Heinrich Wilhelm Dove discovered that when two different frequencies are played into each ear, the brain compromises by producing a third sound known as a binaural beat or tone. In effect, it is a beat frequency. So if 310 Hz were played in one ear, and 300 Hz in the other, the binaural frequency would be 10 Hz. To be effective in therapy, Binaural Beats need to ride on a 'carrier' sound, such as a relaxing or focused musical track, ambient sounds (especially nature), and headphones must be used.

Why is this important? Because when your brain receives Binaural Beats or tones, it naturally goes into a state of relaxation or focus. By adding the right kind of carrier tracks, I set up an optimum platform for adding in special therapeutic and subliminal messages for effective and rapid change that your subconscious can easily absorb.

Isochronic Tones

These are tones, which are evenly spaced and turn on and off quickly. They differ from Binaural Beats as they are created manually by manipulating the frequency, rather than your brain having to do it. The tone you hear is a stable, uninterrupted one as opposed to the more pulsing tone you get with Binaural Beats. However, Isochronic Tones are extremely effective when used in therapeutic recordings because they produce a very strong cortical response in the brain. Using Isochronic Tones means that your brain has to do less work than it does with Binaural Beats, and the biggest advantage of using them is that you do NOT need headphones. This means that you can listen to the MP3s with

Isochronic Tones during the day, while you are working or exercising, without having to block everything else out because of wearing headphones. You can have these recordings on in the background and still get on with other things whilst getting the full effect. Binaural Beats and Isochronic Tones are forms of auditory methods used to facilitate Brainwave Entrainment states.

I use the technology to make my recording effective in getting you into a relaxed and focused state. To ensure you get the best possible listening experience and the most effective therapeutic intervention possible, I add melodic music and auditory inductions that give your subconscious something even more substantial to focus on. Underneath all this, I add a layer of subliminal messages that your subconscious is able to pick up on and interpret into new patterns of behavior that are beneficial and desirable outcomes you have chosen for yourself. This is why my recordings are so seriously powerful. All 5 MP3s in this Law of Attraction Shortcut Secrets Success System are Cogni-Fusion compilations.

The benefits of using BWE with Binaural Beats/Isochronic Tones:

Countless studies have been carried out on the beneficial effects of BWE, and regular use can help the user with a host of issues, including:

- Attracting Wealth and Abundance
- Confidence
- Relaxation
- Memory
- Stress
- Focus
- Pain Management
- Creativity
- Sleep
- ADHD
- Problem Solving
- Learning/Recall
- Substance Addictions
- and more...

The Image below shows brainwave patterns before and after Brainwave Entrainment

Image courtesy of Transparent Corporation©

Understanding Brainwaves: Alpha/Beta/Delta/Theta/Gamma

Everything our brain does, it does using waves. We know this because science has proven it with the use of EEGs and fMRIs as explained above, which measure brainwave activity. There are 5 key brainwaves we need to look at: Alpha, Beta, Delta, Theta, and Gamma.

According to Transparent Corporation©, one of my prime technology partners, brainwave frequencies are as shown as follows:

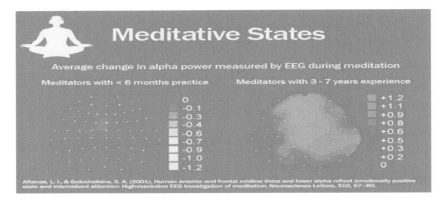

Alpha (8 Hz-12 Hz): Awake, relaxed and not doing very much. Associated with learning new information, creativity, enhanced serotonin release, mood elevation and arousal.

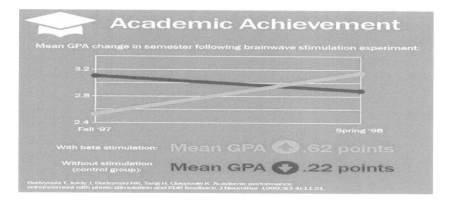

Beta (12 Hz-27 Hz): Awake, alert, normal brainwave stage. Associated with concentration on tasks, focusing, improved attention, problem solving, conscious thinking and learning.

Delta (0.2 Hz-3 Hz: Deep/Deeper relaxation. Associated with pain reduction, endorphin release, euphoria, harmony, balance, production of endogenous opiates (enkephalins) to control pain and reduce anxiety, restful sleep, self-renewal, enhancement, improves memory, learning and problem solving.

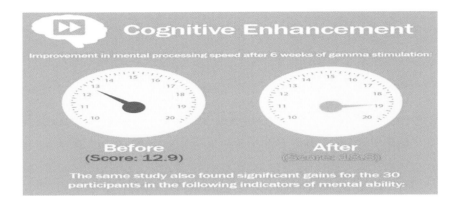

Theta (3 Hz – 8 Hz): Very deep levels of relaxation. Associated with restful/deeper sleep, meditation, inner guidance and intuition, creative ability especially for art, invention, and music. Also used for grounding, meditation, memory, focus, inner peace, emotional healing and mental fatigue.

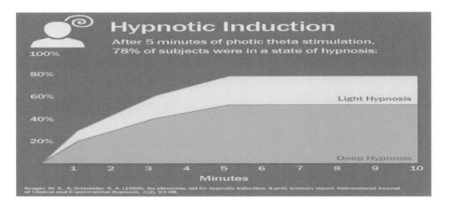

Gamma (27 Hz-100 Hz): Associated with formation of ideas, language, memory, and learning. These are considered 'higher' states, usually only achievable by those who have spent a great deal of time meditating, such as Tibetan Monks.

I incorporate the correct brainwave inducing frequencies to obtain the desired brainwave state. My bonus meditation recording, for example, uses Delta Hz frequencies to take you into a deeply relaxed state. I have added an additional layer of power-packed suggestions so that even if you meditate on something entirely of your own choosing, your subconscious will be wide open to the deep layer of Subliminal Suggestions. You can simply double the benefits of your meditation sessions with this method.

Subliminal Messages

Subliminal messages in audio are recorded at a low level, below the sound of the carrier music and Binaural Beats or Isochronic Tones. Your conscious mind is unable to hear them or make the words out if they are at 'whisper' level. However it has been proven in clinical trials that the subconscious is able to hear at a level lower than normal auditory capability.

Some people are sceptical about subliminal recordings, saying that if they can't hear the words, how do they know they are there? This is a fair question, but a large body of research shows the subconscious can indeed hear words and sounds not audible to the conscious ear.

It is well known that some people were able to hear words that had been spoken whilst in a coma, even though they were unable to move or respond in any way. And we all know dogs can hear a whistle inaudible to the human ear - the principle is somewhat similar; dogs have a better, more acute sense of hearing than humans but the pitch of the whistle is at a much higher frequency that they can hear, but humans cannot. Your subconscious is able to hear at a frequency that your ears cannot. On some of our recordings, you can hear the 'whisper' of words, but not quite make out what is being said. Rest assured however, your subconscious can.

Their efficacy has been proven in many studies, for example:

"Kaser, V.A. "The Effects of an Auditory Subliminal Perception Message Upon the Production of Images and Dreams". Journal of Nervous and Mental Disease."

"A group of subjects were exposed to an auditory subliminal message to study whether messages could be transmitted subliminally. The subliminal message was produced by speeding up a message that was sung until it could not be consciously understood, and was mixed with a normal music recording. Another group of subjects was exposed to the normal music recording without the subliminal recording.

Both groups were asked to produce a pre-test drawing before and immediately after the tapes were played as well as a drawing of any dreams they might have that night.

Analysis of all the drawings by two art therapists showed a significant difference between the dream drawings and imagery drawings of the experimental and the control group. When the drawings were examined, the effects of the subliminal message could be seen.

The research findings suggest that the subconscious is able to perceive a recorded verbal message that cannot be consciously heard, proving the existence of subliminal perception."

Another article in Time Magazine in September 1979 entitled: 'Secret Voices: Messages that manipulate" reported:

"Basically a sound mixer like those used by disco deejays, the box mingles bland music with subliminal anti-theft messages ("I am honest. I will not steal"). Repeated rapidly - 9,000 times an hour -- and at very low volume, the words are barely audible to shoppers and employees. However they do register in some deep recess of the brain and apparently influence behavior. About 50 department stores in the U.S. and Canada have installed the devices to reduce shoplifting and employee theft. One undisclosed East Coast chain is said to have cut the number of thefts by 37%, for a saving of $600,000, during a nine-month trial. The device also seems to be catching on in other businesses."

My Belief About Subliminal Messages

I firmly believe, and my own experience has proven, that NOT being able to hear the affirmations being said has a massive advantage over knowing what is being said. Once your conscious mind is aware the inner saboteur will immediately get to work on clinging to the old habits and patterns.

Look at the image below and see if can find the subliminal message in it. You may have seen this logo hundreds of times, as I had, but never consciously noticed it. I'll reveal it at the end of this e- Book in case you can't find it.

Try NOT to notice the hidden message in the FedEx logo once you know what it is – it is virtually impossible now because you know it is there. I have experienced the inner saboteur many times with people during therapy. So I deliberately DO NOT list the details of the subliminal therapy – it can be counter-productive.

I believe that once you listen to them, you will soon understand the remarkable power of your own subconscious mind. My breakthrough Cogni-Fusion recordings integrate all of these techniques, creating a profoundly different and highly effective Audio System for rapid personal success. You don't need to force yourself to listen to what is being said. Just let your subconscious over and do the work for you.

If, however, you would like to have the affirmation scripts, you can request them from me personally. In compliance with British Standards in Clinical Hypnotherapy Practice, I keep copies of all my scripts on file. E-mail me at

mailto:mariaprivatemembers@gmail.com

Your Conscious Mind – Left Brain

Your conscious mind is your waking, thinking, logical, reasoning, analytical self. It is the part of you that knows how to get out of bed in the morning, get you dressed and ready for the day. Whilst many of the actions that you carry out during the day are 'automatic', you nevertheless make a conscious decision to get out of bed in the morning, to eat breakfast, to get into your car and drive to work. Your conscious mind is the part that is above the surface, where your 'active brain' resides. It is with you now consciously reading this. Typically your 'left brain' is held to be responsible for short-term memory, logical thinking, critical thinking and willpower.

Your Subconscious mind – Right Brain

The subconscious (which means 'below the threshold') is often likened to an iceberg - the tip you see above the water is the conscious mind, whereas the massive block beneath the surface is where all the action is really taking place. Your subconscious is also often compared to a computer's hard drive, where a mind-boggling amount of data is stored. It is estimated that your brain can store anywhere between 3 and 1000 terabytes of data. That's a heck of a lot of brainpower processing. Typically your 'right brain' is held to be responsible for your beliefs, emotions, values, intuition, habits, imagination, long-term memory and protective/instinctive reactions. In truth, no one is wholly left or right brained, as we all use both parts of our brain, but most people do have a dominant side.

Why Is My Subconscious Mind So Important In All This?

These data are gathered from the moment you are born, and every day for the rest of your life, information is being collected and stored in this powerhouse of knowledge. Your subconscious is responsible for everything you do without awareness or having to think about – breathing, sleeping, walking, moving, healing, digestion, and much more. It is where all your mental programming is stored. This encompasses your thoughts, feelings, emotions, reactions, preferences, memories, dreams, ideals, desires... the list is endless. It is often noted that we only use 10% of our subconscious / brain's capacity. The other 90% is an untapped treasure trove waiting for you to access it. You just need the right key. What is critical to understand about your subconscious is that because all your original programming is stored in here, negative things that happened when you were a child, or when you were unaware of them, could have been picked up and now those negative programs are still playing in your mind, like an old movie.

Your subconscious is causing you to act and react in accordance with those old programs for two reasons: One, it thinks that it is protecting you from some kind of harm or threat, and two, it has no concept of time. I doesn't understand that something you heard or were told when you were five or ten or twelve years old is not necessarily true, not necessarily your reality, and absolutely not necessary to your life as you live it – or rather want to live it - today. It just doesn't know this. And until you can 're-educate' it, by bringing the software of your mind up to date with what you really do want in your life now, it will continue with the negative loop and you can battle it with all the anger, frustration, negative inner talk, criticism, bargaining and willpower you can throw at it – but it won't change a thing, because your subconscious is in charge. It's the boss! That is why reprogramming your brain with Cogni-Fusion is so effective - because it enables you to bring your brain's software right up to date with where you want to be, right now.

Understanding Repetition

It is also important to note that repetition is key in reprogramming your mind. Your subconscious likes to hear the same thing over and over so that it 'sticks'. It is one of the reasons repetition is used in key learning tasks, such as multiplication tables or languages. Think about anything you've had to learn in your life. How many times did you have to physically do it (think tying your shoelaces... or learning to drive) before it became so ingrained in your brain that you didn't have to consciously think about it any more? Your brain needs lots of repetitions for the new programming to be laid down via neural pathways. For this reason you will be hearing a lot of repetition in the MP3s as this is part of the technique used to firmly embed the changes into your subconscious.

Hypnosis

Many people are fearful of hypnosis, incorrectly thinking that they will lose control or worse, be 'under the control' of the Hypnotherapist. In fact, nothing could be further from the truth, and a well-known statement that all therapists will attest to is that 'all hypnosis is self-hypnosis'.

How do you get hypnotized? A trained Hypnotherapist will begin by talking in a way that relaxes you, often using music, then therapeutic techniques such as NLP, positive affirmations, ego strengthening, guided visualizations, various therapeutic interventions and post hypnotic suggestions, to help you eliminate negative behavior patterns and replace them with more beneficial ones. My System utilizes all these techniques as well as the additional layers of subliminal programming and Brainwave Entrainment. There is no System out there more powerful than this.

You cannot be hypnotized against your will. You have to allow it to happen. Furthermore you can hear everything that is being said (with the exception of course, of the subliminal parts) and can recall the entire session should you choose to. You are always fully in control and aware of what is going on.

The beauty of listening to my recordings is there is no third party involved, so any fears you might harbor about losing control will be completely absent, as you are choosing when, where and how to listen.

Hypnotic Induction

This is at the beginning of a Hypnotherapy session, where the therapist talks you gently into a state of relaxation. There are numerous techniques to achieve this, including full body relaxation, deepeners and so on. My recordings use a variety of inductions that put you completely in control of where you want to 'be' during the process – a mental, imaginary process that gives you unlimited potentialities. This method of using variety ensures that you are never bored listening to the same script over and over.

Post-hypnotic Suggestion

These are positive suggestions/affirmations that a therapist will generally use during your Hypnotherapy session with the aim of your subconscious mind recalling them and acting on them effortlessly after the session. These will always be positive, life affirming suggestions aimed at helping you reach your goals more quickly.

Neuro Linguistic Programming (NLP)

Very briefly, NLP comprises three key components of human communication: neurological, language (linguistic) and programming. The neurological system regulates our bodily function, language deals with communication between ourselves and others, and programming deals with the kinds of models of the world we create.

For our purposes here, it is important to note three key elements of NLP that we use to make sense of our world. Understanding these will greatly enhance your ability to visualize when you start listening to the MP3s. We have 5 senses – 5 modalities with which we perceive the world:

- Seeing (Visual)
- Hearing (Auditory)
- Feeling (Kinesthetic)
- Tasting (Gustatory)
- Olfactory (Smell)

We all have them but most people will have a dominant mode of processing information within the first three above. For example:

If you are a predominantly visual person, you are likely to say:

"I see what you mean" or 'That looks good to me" Or, 'I can just picture that."

If you are a predominantly auditory person, you are likely to say:

"That sounds good to me", or "I hear what you are saying" or 'That rings a bell".

If you are predominantly Kinesthetic, you are likely to say:

"I feel happy about that" or "My gut instinct is…"or "Let's touch base".

We use gustatory and olfactory language in everyday speech less often, but they are still used. It is still common to hear people say:

'Food for thought', 'I smell a rat', 'I need time to digest that' and so on, and you will often hear expressions like "What a sweet thing to say" or "She has such a sour disposition'.

The importance of understanding your primary modality is this: when you start asking yourself questions about what changes you'd like to have in your life, and begin writing them down, it is helpful to know what your primary modality is because when you plan your creative visualization, for example, you will know that if you are primarily Kinesthetic, you should concentrate on how you feel and what you want to feel more of. If you are primarily visual, you should concentrate on conjuring up visual imagery. It can be quite fun. My 'Creative Visualization - Nature Trail' bonus MP3 will guide you through this process and help hone your visualizing skills.

Creative Visualization

In 1978, Shakti Gawain published her seminal work, 'Creative Visualization' and launched what was virtually an unheard of concept at the time. The book has since sold over 6 million copies in more than 30 languages, and for many it remains the most cherished work on the subject to this day. Many, many more books have been written about the technique, and thousands of 'gurus' attest to its power. So what is creative visualization, exactly?

Creative Visualization is the art of using your imagination as vividly as you can to feed your subconscious with images of the wonderful things you desire in your life. Generally it is best to settle down, relax and let your mind wander into your visualization of choice. The more vividly you can see, hear and feel in your imagination the greater the impact on your subconscious mind, as it does not know the difference between real and imagined. When you vividly imagine something regularly, your subconscious thinks it is real, and helps move you towards the reality of making it real in your life. I have included a Creative Visualization MP3 within the bonus pack, so you will discover exactly how to do this.

Positive Affirmations

Positive affirmations are your list of 'feel good' things you'd like to be, have or do. How positive affirmations are phrased is very important. You should always state the positive outcome and never use negative terms. So for example if you want to lose weight, a positive affirmation would be 'I am losing weight easily' rather than 'I want to lose weight'. Instead of 'I am debt free' – use 'my bills are paid easily and on time'. Affirmations should be phrased in the present tense, as if the affirmation is already a reality.

All positive affirmations in my recordings use carefully structured language to ensure the focus is always on the positive outcomes you wish to achieve. These are blended in with Subliminal Suggestions for change. Affirmations are great to have around and I recommend typing up your favorites and sticking them up in your home or office (or both) where you will see them often. This helps reinforce your desired outcomes.

Positive affirmations, in and of themselves, will not always work... because simply overlaying positive affirmations on top of serious limiting-beliefs is not enough to counteract the strength of the 'true' limiting beliefs that you might currently be holding. This is why I have so extensively covered limiting beliefs and how to change them in this book. Once you do that, positive affirmations will add great strength to your new beliefs.

All 5 MP3s in this System are Cogni-Fusion compilations packed with Subliminal Suggestions, dual voice auditory relaxation, therapy and positive affirmations for rapid and effective change.

Relaxation Techniques

Sitting or lying down anywhere, resting, sunbathing, dozing, daydreaming, listening to mellow music – these are all relaxation techniques and most of us do some or all of them regularly. Focused relaxation techniques are those that talk you into a completely relaxed and comfortable state. I use this technique in all my Cogni-Fusion MP3s, which are designed for night-time listening (excluding the Bonus Powerhouse Five, which is specifically designed for daytime listening).

Meditation

Yes, I know, you probably think of Yogis and Buddhist Monks sitting cross-legged for hours on end, contemplating the universe... and you are simply not supple enough to get one leg across one thigh, never mind both of them! Me neither. The good news is that there are many different ways to meditate and you do not have to tie yourself up in Yogic knots to do them. But why bother with this in the first place, you ask, when you could be doing more important things? The benefits of meditation are legion, and you need to understand that everything in your life can improve significantly if you get into the habit of regular meditation. All the books I have referred to bring up the importance of meditation and its connection to the Universal Laws and manifesting your desires every time.

Some people believe that meditation has to be a long and drawn out process. This is not the case. Needless to say, the more you put in the more you get out, but I would always advise a newcomer to start with very short sessions, maybe ten to fifteen minutes – or even as little as two, and as you become more experienced at meditating you may wish to lengthen the sessions. Here are just a few of the well-documented and scientifically proven benefits of meditation:

- reduces stress
- reduces blood pressure
- improves digestion
- improves sex/libido
- helps overcome anxiety/depression
- increases brain size/thickness
- strengthens brain cell connections
- decreases pain
- improves sleep
- improves immune system
- relaxes you and thereby reduces tension

In addition to that, meditation is frequently referred to as the 'gateway to higher consciousness'; put another way, it simply means getting in touch with your inner self – i.e. your subconscious. When you make this connection, and link it to how it can help you manifest the life of your dreams, it can suddenly take on a whole new meaning for you.

So I hope that helps you to understand the science and psychology that has gone into creating Cogni-Fusion Mind Expansion Technology. Now let's look at what might be going on in your life that is preventing you from achieving the financial, emotional, physical and spiritual wealth that you are seeking.

CHAPTER 2

Shortcut Secrets: The 7 Critical Blocks to Your Law of Attraction Success:

Why understanding these blocks is essential to your Law of Attraction success

1. **Self-Limiting Beliefs**
2. **Self-Sabotage**
3. **Expecting Diamonds from Dust: Unrealistic Expectations**
4. **'Shiny Object Syndrome'**
5. **Lack of Patience**
6. **Blame Culture**
7. **Not Committing to Your Personal Success**

We are very often our own worst enemies in more ways than one. I'd like to dissect each of these critical blocks that many of us have struggled with. Let's start with the most damaging one of all.

Key Block No. 1 - Self-limiting Beliefs

Beliefs: what are they in general?

Why your current belief system could be preventing you from succeeding and how listening to my multi-layered Cogni-Fusion MP3 will help you blast your self-limiting beliefs into oblivion.

We all have beliefs about everything. Your beliefs begin forming in childhood when you pick up on what you hear your parents and siblings talking about. As you progress through school, college, university, your first job, you continue to form and develop your beliefs. Your social circle, media and education play a huge part in shaping your beliefs, as does other more deeply ingrained conditioned thinking from your cultural, religious, political and socio-economic background.

Beliefs are necessary for survival. You need them as frames of reference to help you move through life, and as they become ingrained in your subconscious, they take root and become your reality. Most, or many, of your beliefs are true, accurate and help protect you as you go through life. However, not ALL of them are. Many of them are out-dated and working against your true desires.

Self-limiting Beliefs: what are they?

How discovering your own deeply hidden beliefs can free your mind and re-program it for success.

Simply put, self-limiting beliefs are those negative thoughts that float about in your head and prevent you from being, doing or achieving life-changing things because you:

(A)   Subconsciously fear failure, hurt, pain or deprivation, or often all of these. Your subconscious beliefs protect you from any kind of harm, but conflict arises when your conscious, logical mind wants to change. To become wealthy and successful, for example, lose weight, stop smoking, exercise more, feel more confident etc., but your subconscious does not, because it thinks that it is protecting you and forces you to continue with the behavior that in fact, no longer serves you and is in opposition to what you desire in your life now;

(B)   Believe you are undeserving in some way. You may lack self-confidence, have low-self esteem, as well as some of those blocks mentioned in the 7 Key Blocks that are preventing you from succeeding.

So for example – think of any 'negative' habit or thought you regularly indulge in against your better judgment. You know it is bad for you, it is not what you want to do or think, but your subconscious has other ideas. Because it believes that the habit or thought is serving you in some way due to long-standing negative programming. No matter how much you argue with yourself on a conscious level that you do not want to continue with the habit or thought, you can't stop whatever it is you are trying to resist or change. Your subconscious loves these habits/thoughts because they are comforting and satisfying, having been with you for so long. It thinks you need the habits or thoughts now because you have always needed them.

Once you identify a self-limiting belief, ask yourself these questions:

- Does this belief serve or help me in any way? (Think about it carefully.)
- Are your thoughts/beliefs valid?
- Are they relevant?
- Are they even true?
- Who says so?
- Why?

Let's say you do not think you deserve success. Ask yourself these questions:

- Why do you think that?
- Why are you less deserving of great success than the next person?
- Is that belief working for your best interests?

- What value does it have for you in any way?
- What would it be like to let that belief go?
- What belief could you install in your mind instead?

Very often we act and think automatically because we have been programmed to do so for so long, we simply keep playing the same old negative loop in our minds. And most of the time, it's negative thinking!

Dr Robert Anthony, in his book 'Betting on Yourself', cites this interesting piece of research:

"It has been estimated that by the age of 18, the average person has heard the word 'No' over 150,000 times. Researchers have estimated that approximately 75% of what we think about is thought of in a negative, self-defeating way. Year after year we continue to be inundated with negative messages that gradually become part of our life script. Not surprisingly, we begin doing it ourselves on a daily basis. We begin chipping away at our confidence and our self-esteem."

So, we inadvertently become our own worst enemies. We stop asking relevant questions like those above that can illuminate just how useless and debilitating some of our thoughts, feelings and beliefs are. This is particularly true if the accompanying feeling or thought is shrouded in negative energy. You feel miserable, depressed, bad, sad and unhappy because negative energy is heavy. It drags you down, and sometimes you do not even realize it. Negative energy is bad for you – this is the first thing you need to fully understand

and conquer if you are to achieve the success your heart truly desires.

If you are manifesting bad situations in your life, then believe me the generator of these bad situations is your own negative energy. The section on Law of Attraction covers this in more detail. The good news however, is you CAN realize and release the negatives and deal with every single one of your self-limiting beliefs. And it is easier than you think once you understand the underlying causes and get a grasp on how your subconscious works.

My System will show you, step-by-step, how to identify and then release your self-limiting beliefs. You will be wiping the slate clean and starting to alter the frequency of your thoughts. By doing this, you are sending out a whole new vibe to the universe. And the experiences you manifest will change.

How do I identify my self-limiting Beliefs?

How discovering your own deeply hidden beliefs can free your mind and re-program it for success.

Now, this is where your sparkling new notebook or journal comes in. The best way is to keep that notebook and pen handy. Then, start listening to your internal dialogue. Tuning in to your mental chatter is vitally important. How do you talk to yourself on any given time or day? What are you saying, exactly? What feelings come up when you have a thought related to the issue you want to change? Start writing your thoughts down as soon as you have finished reading this book.

Say for example, you want to get rich. As soon as you have that thought, a deeper, underlying 'voice' might say:

- Money is bad
- Rich people are evil
- You have to be born rich
- I'm never going to be rich
- I don't have any talent to get rich
- I have always struggled
- I don't deserve to be rich
- I'd have to work impossible hours to get rich
- I'd have to sacrifice everything to get rich

Or you want to find the perfect partner, your dream soul mate, but every time the thought comes to mind, you think:

- My relationships always go wrong
- Nobody will ever love me
- I'm not good enough for anyone to love
- I'm a disaster with relationships
- I'm so unlucky in love

… and so on.

If you are thinking along these or similar lines, you are absolutely working the Law of Attraction... you are getting (attracting) exactly that which you are constantly thinking about and re-affirming with your negative internal dialogue.

However, that can easily be changed. Tell yourself right now, that today is the day you are going to let go and move on! You are not going to wallow in self-pity, self-loathing or self-derogation any more. You know the saying 'Enough is enough'? Say it to yourself now! And mean it. Then get ready to let go and move on!

Once you realize the past is truly in the past, that it does not need to hold you back if you are willing to let go, you can free yourself from so much negative baggage that simply does not serve you anymore, in any way. Releasing & letting go of your past is incredibly liberating. When you truly realize all that matters is now, this very moment, EVERY moment, you can find a totally new sense of freedom within.

I believe that truly letting go, along with forgiving yourself and others for all past perceived or real transgressions, are two of the most important components of living a life of happiness, joy and fulfilment.

So in your mind now, your thoughts might go something like this: 'I'll never be rich because you have to be born rich'. Or "I'll never love again because it leads to being hurt.' Using NLP techniques, we will work through these negative patterns and allow you to change them. So for example, you can start thinking: 'I used to think I'd never be rich because you have to be born rich, but now I KNOW that is not true. I now choose to be rich'. Or: 'I may have been hurt in the past, but I let that go and I know I can be happy in future. I choose to find a wonderful person who is perfect for me.'

You can think like this at a surface level, but when you start to teach these true desires to your subconscious mind, you will see and feel an immediate shift in your psyche. Another example is: 'I am never going to succeed at this...whatever it is.... because.... fill in the gap yourself.

Now ask yourself what is the belief that is holding you back? Why do you think this?

- Because you are not smart enough?
- Experienced enough?
- Lucky enough?
- Deserving enough?
- Beautiful enough?

Whatever it is, identify it, and write it down. Then when you have the thought again, you immediately change it to: 'I used to think that I'd never succeed in... whatever... but now I KNOW that is not true and I choose to think... something much more positive... instead. Write this new positive statement down after each new limiting belief that you identify. Do this until you have written down every objection you can come up with.

And remember to ask yourself those pivotal questions mentioned earlier: above.

- Are your thoughts/beliefs valid?
- Are they relevant?
- Are they even true?
- Who says so?
- On what foundations are these thoughts/beliefs based?

If they do not enhance your life in any way, think about letting them go and what freedom from this kind of emotional baggage would do for you. Another quick, useful tip is to catch yourself as soon as you hear the negative thought and immediately say 'STOP!' Picture a big red 'Stop' sign as you do this. Then re-frame the thought with a new, empowering one as suggested above. Keep doing this. You will find that soon your negative thinking will be less and less as you begin to systematically discard all your old self-limiting beliefs. These outcomes will be much more effective once you start listening to my MP3s.

Dr Joe Vitale, in his book, 'Attract Money Now', offers some great advice in this area, and I advise you to do the following 3 steps:

1. "Reflect on the three key limiting beliefs and write down which ones you perceive to be true for you at the moment.

2. Write down the opposite of the limiting beliefs and reflect on what it feels like to deserve and enjoy money. (I'd add 'let your imagination run riot' here!)

3. Consider other beliefs that may be limiting you from attracting money, and reflect on the opposite of those beliefs, so you know you deserve money now."

This exercise can take a few days to a week so it is important (and easier) to just write down exactly what comes out. Do this every day for a week or more depending on how many of them you have stored up and be honest with yourself. This is absolutely essential.

Every time you say or think 'I can't because...' or 'I won't because...' there is almost certainly a self-limiting, fear-based belief behind that thought. Tune in to your personal dialogue. Get it out in the open. It is your truth that matters here, so tell it like it is.

We often tend to avoid the truth in ourselves because facing it hurts, but until you peel away the layers and get to the truth, you will never be able to find true joy and abundance.

Once the week is up, go over your notes and look for patterns. What are the key points that keep coming up? These will be the first thoughts that come to mind when you are about to indulge again in the behavior or thought pattern you want to change but can't. Listen to the amazing way your subconscious provides a plethora of excuses, reasons and justifications for why you simply MUST keep thinking this way/doing these things. But let me tell you something - it is time to outsmart your subconscious for once.

This technique is surprisingly effective in helping you to identify the root causes associated with these unwanted thoughts/habits. It is no less effective in helping you understand why you have other emotional issues, such as anxiety or self-sabotage, or are blocking your own path to wealth and success.

Sometimes, the simple act of listening to your internal dialogue over a week can be enough, but for some people there might be a little additional work to do.

So here is a method to help you get started.

What areas of your life do you really want/need/desire to change?

'The Top 10 Categories' for Change Analysis

Take a quick inventory: On a scale of 1 to 10 — 10 being tops, where would you rank yourself in the following 10 categories. Your ideal score would be 100 if all 10 categories are applicable to you but they may not be. Stay-at-home mums, for example, may not be at all concerned with careers. Just tot up the ones that apply to you.

It's really easy to do this and figure out how happy you are with each. And super-quick to identify where you are least happy. This simple exercise showed me very quickly where the big dips were in my life. So now, note these down in your journal and tot up your scores.

- Relationships (work)
- Career
- Family
- Friends
- Finances
- Health
- Personal development
- Hobbies / Social life
- Life balance
- Spiritual Life

As you reflect on each category, put them under a metaphorical microscope, and be brutally honest with yourself about each point (no point in lying to you, right?).

When you've done that, number them in order of the biggest problem down to the smallest.

Then, start with the big one. Put the others aside for now, because you're going to identify what it is in that area you are unhappy about. It is often the case that when you sort out one problem, others disappear of their own accord. For example, let's say you are really unhappy in your job. You come home stressed and miserable every day and take your frustration out on your partner or family. They in turn get upset and as a result, the relationships become strained. Everyone feels bad.

Now let's say you change jobs, find one you love... suddenly you become a much nicer person to be around, you're back to being your normal happy self... everyone notices. Relationships are much better.

But back to the problem. So, the biggie is staring up at you from its top slot on your journal. Time to get to work on it.

Questions you need to answer first (and be sure to write your answers down in your journal because everything you feel is important to note):

- What do I dislike about this situation?
- Why do I dislike it?
- Why do I feel like this?
- How long have I felt this way?
- Is it due to external influences or is it just inside me?
- How exactly does this feeling affect me? (eg: Am I angry, frustrated, miserable...?)
- What have I done to change/improve the situation?
- Do I truly WANT to change/improve the situation?
- What is stopping me from changing/improving the situation?
- Why is this stopping me?
- What am I really afraid of?
- What is so bad about that?

- Am I really in an impossible situation, destined to spend the rest of my life in misery?
- Am I totally blameless in this?
- Am I totally helpless in this?
- Do I own any part of this?
- How responsible am I for this?
- Does this make me a bad person?

Do you see how these questions once you start can lead you down all kinds of interesting paths? This exercise is much more powerful than it looks because it forces you to answer honestly, and the answers that come up are generally very illuminating.

Once you've totally exhausted every Q&A you can think of, you're ready to move on to the next stage. Ok, go have a coffee break first... you deserve it!

Ok, now it's time to start looking for solutions. Don't worry about the reality of the solutions just yet... just brainstorm to see what comes up. There IS a solution to every problem and you probably know that already, deep down.

If you are one of those people who immediately throws your hands up in the air and cries: "Oh I can't do this, that, the other because, because, because….' STOP. This is negative self-talk – it's self-limiting belief in action. Go back and ask yourself these questions:

What if...

What if I could do something about this? What would that something be?

What if I DON'T do something about this? Where will that leave me?

How about...

How about I research this and see what kind of solutions I can find?

How about I check with family/friends/colleagues/Pastor/Chat Forums/the Internet – to see what solutions other people have found?

Maybe I could...

Other people have done this, maybe I could...

What would...

What would my ideal solution be to fix this situation?

What do I need to do to make that happen?

Do I...

Do I have the courage to do that?

Do I have the skills to do that?

Do I have the knowledge/know how to do that?

If you answer NO to all the above 'Do I?' questions, go back up to the 'What if/How about/Maybe I' sections again. There IS a way out of every situation, no matter how bleak. You have to allow yourself to believe this, and then go about finding the way out.

Once you've gone through these exercises, you should have a very clear picture of where the stumbling blocks are and what you can do to change your situation. Almost certainly you will identify one or even several self-limiting beliefs. Once you have those pegged, you will have some seriously good tools to start working with. Now, you may not change your life overnight, but you will have placed the all-important, if small, seed of change in your mind, and your subconscious will go to work on finding a solution or solutions, for you.

Then, my 'Blast your Self-Limiting Beliefs' Cogni-Fusion MP3 will take you through the process of releasing and letting go of all those beliefs that are no longer serving your best interests. It is an extremely effective therapeutic technique that will prime your subconscious mind for the new powerful reprogramming that will lead you to the life of your dreams – the Law of Attraction Shortcut Secrets will start being revealed to your subconscious mind. Once you do this you will have the motivation and inner driving force to propel you forward to find big solutions and to make them happen.

Realize and accept that you own your self-limiting beliefs

It is important to fully understand that all of your self-limiting beliefs stem from your subconscious mind's fierce desire to protect you from harm, so acknowledging this is the first step to eliminating them and rebuilding a better set of beliefs. They are your beliefs, no matter how, why or when they were formed, no matter that they are no longer serving your best interests. You do that by simply saying 'Thank you' to your inner self. 'Thank you for trying to always protect me.' And mean it when you say it. Then get ready to move on, and fast.

Self-limiting Beliefs: my advice

Do the groundwork. Keep your notebook handy, and jot down every time you hear yourself saying or thinking negative thoughts. Remember the 'STOP' sign. This will give you incredible ammunition to work with once you start listening to my MP3: Blast your Self-Limiting Beliefs because you will KNOW exactly what you need to eliminate.

Self-limiting Beliefs: my steepest learning curve

I was shocked when I first carried out this exercise to realize how much negative self-talk was going on in my head. It was awful. I thought everyone else was better, smarter, more switched on, than I was. One day, someone I respected said something that hit home for me. "Maria" this friend said, "everyone has to start somewhere, and there will always be someone more qualified, more established, more talented and richer than you are, but there are also millions more who are much less of all those things than you are. Know who you are… what you want to be, then go out and be that person". I would give you the same advice. You create your reality. Make it the reality you truly desire.

Key Block No 2: Self Sabotage / Inner Saboteur

How learning to recognize this inner demon is the next most important step in your journey to reprogramming your mind for phenomenal success.

This is one we ALL need to be aware of. It is lurking in every single one of us at some point. You start out with the best of intentions, but the 'bad guy' just wheedles back in and derails your good intentions. It is that part of you that drags you back down into the behavior or thought process you are trying to escape from. The Inner Saboteur is very closely linked to self-limiting beliefs, so it is important to bear this in mind when you consider those, and you will have the ammunition needed to fight them all and win. You will be able to build a strong case for convincing your subconscious that you are now ready to release all these negative little gremlins, and replace them with new, beneficial beliefs. Beliefs that will serve you better, put you more in control and add greater value to your life and your health.

Common forms of self-sabotage are procrastination, burying emotions with alcohol and drugs, and of course, comfort eating. Think about your past attempts to succeed at something – what was it that derailed you? Chances are that was your inner saboteur at work.

Eliminating Self Limiting Beliefs & Silencing your Inner Saboteur

How my technique can finally free you from your self-limiting beliefs and banish your inner saboteur

My special Cogni-Fusion MP3 recording is specifically aimed at blasting ALL of your negative, self-limiting beliefs and inner saboteur into oblivion - no matter how many of them you have, no matter why, and no matter how long you have held them. Your inner saboteur will be silenced once and for all, and once this happens, my powerful, proven NLP techniques in the subsequent MP3s will put a new set of successful thinking strategies into your mind. It will be as if you have wiped the slate clean and made it ready to write a new program onto the neural pathways of your brain. To make this process even more effective, underlying the therapy is a plethora of new, positive beliefs that your subconscious will be ready and eager to accept as your new reality.

Self-sabotage/inner saboteur: my advice

As with identifying your self-limiting beliefs, get to know your inner saboteur intimately. What does the voice say? Or is it more of a 'feeling'... one that makes you want to do something that you are consciously trying to change? Keep looking for your inner saboteur. Question yourself constantly, to get to the bottom of what's lurking inside you.

Self-sabotage/inner saboteur: my steepest learning curve

I had so many inner saboteurs whizzing around inside me, at times I felt really low and worthless. I would eat too much... drink too much... feel down and depressed because I didn't think I could change what was going on inside me. Foolish thoughts indeed! Once I understood the Universal Laws, and found the method of delivering the wonderful truths to my subconscious mind, literally everything changed for the better. I stopped drinking, lost 20 lbs., and woke up to the truth that I can control my thoughts, and therefore attract the good things I want in my life. Things just keep getting better and better for me. They will for you too. My MP3 'Blast Your Self-Limiting Beliefs' also deals with your inner saboteur.

Key Block No 3: Diamonds from Dust: Unrealistic Expectations

How taking a reality check will keep you grounded and working steadily towards success

Ok, before I get into this section, have a look at the image below. Would you consider yourself lucky if you found this? Would you even know what it was? Never having seen one like this before, I wouldn't have! But read through this section, and I'll share a surprise with you at the end!

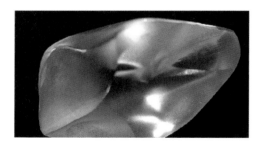

When you decide to start a program or course, no matter what it is, you need to plan it out and take time to make the plan work. You need to have a systematic strategy in place, one that you stick to and are prepared to put effort into. Even if the effort is as simple as correcting your negative inner talk and listening to a very pleasant recording once a day.

If we are not prepared to put in a little bit of effort to greatly improve ourselves, then how can we expect to see positive changes? The answer is: We can't. I know this because I was guilty of negligence myself. I know how busy life gets for everyone, and there are always so many other things to do, so many demands to meet, that we all too often put our own personal needs aside. This is a big mistake. It wasn't until I really decided to monitor my progress that things began to change. I decided to work the Law of Attraction and make it work for me. I decided to dedicate time to it, come hell or high water. That determination led me to achieving so much more than I could ever have imagined, including losing 20lbs weight, curing my insomnia, setting up www.atuneu.com and subsequently mariamcmahon.com, and creating the Cogni-Fusion System. All of this I achieved within one year. I'd call that big Law of Attraction Shortcut Secret strategy! More hugely exciting things are happening for me right now - but I'll save those for another time.

Too many people start a program and expect miracles overnight. They have done very little 'prospecting' and are expecting to find 'diamonds from dust', as I have come to think of it. Give yourself a 'reality check' and evaluate your true efforts against your actual progress. There is always a direct correlation and if you are brutally honest with yourself, you'll see it. Then you can hone in on the areas where you can make the changes needed to steer you towards your success.

Diamonds from dust: my advice

Once you buy a program, study it carefully and then just do it. Set aside specific time slots for your continued personal development 'learning' – this can be evenings or weekends, but do not neglect it. 30 minutes at least, per day.

One piece of advice I would give you is to stop watching TV. I stopped watching TV a long time ago. The news is 95% bad (negative), the commercials I can live without and much of what is on TV is a waste of time. If you're a big TV fan, consider what you could do with the time you spend watching TV instead. In fact, do a quick calculation now of how many hours you really do spend in front of the TV each week. Go on, be honest, and see if you are as shocked at how many hours that adds up to as many of my clients usually are! So, maybe you could try cutting down and watching only programs that you really do enjoy or benefit from rather than watching mindless drivel that does nothing to drive you towards your goal of creating the life you truly desire and deserve.

Diamonds from dust: my steepest learning curve

I spent years reading wonderful books on the Law of Attraction, self-help and therapy. There was nothing wrong with any of them and they have all helped me gain a huge knowledge base. They all contained pearls of wisdom, nuggets of gold, but I was so busy 'prospecting' that I couldn't really see the value. It was not until I started really applying the Laws to my every-moment thinking that everything began to change. You have to walk the talk. Then you really will start to see amazing changes in your life.

And the picture I asked you about at the beginning of this section? Well that turned out to be The Silver Moon Diamond that was found at Crater of Diamonds State Park in Arkansas, US, by treasure hunters Melissa and Kenny Oliver. The flawless, 2.44 carat diamond, after cutting, was valued at US$21,639." Not a bad little diamond to find among the dust!

Key Block No 4: Shiny Object Syndrome

Why you need to be choosy when picking your 'Shiny Object'

Every single day new products are landing in your inbox with promises of untold wealth, miracle cures, magic 'make-money-for-doing-nothing' promises, and the 'next big thing' that you simply have to have. This situation is not going away anytime soon. You will never be able to keep up with even a fraction of it, and you will just end up wasting more and more of your precious time chasing elusive dreams that end up lost somewhere in your inbox. Again this is an area where a reality check can come in handy. Evaluate yourself. Are you trying something new every week and hoping that one of them will provide the elusive solution you are seeking, moving on so quickly you have not given the most recent one a fair chance? See I know all this goes on because I've done it! So, you have to stop all that or you will just end up running around in circles... getting absolutely nowhere. Set yourself a goal, one key objective, and determine that you will stick with it until you have reached the place you want to be in respect to that issue. Make it a reasonable goal, one that will stretch your limits, but no so big that it's outrageously unobtainable. Leave the big guns until you have successfully mastered a few of the smaller ones.

Shiny object syndrome: my advice

One lady I came across recently admitted she'd spent $12,000 on 'Shiny Objects' and hadn't made any progress from her investments. Do not let this happen to you. Stick with the program you have bought into; study it, work it, believe in it, and do not drop it half way through in favor of something else. Give it your full attention. Do not get side-tracked as this only diverts you from your chosen product and simply wastes your time, your money and dilutes your efforts.

Shiny object syndrome: my steepest learning curve

All that glitters is not gold

I am almost embarrassed to admit how much of a glutton for 'Shiny Objects' I was. And I have also spent thousands of dollars (and I mean thousands!) on promised glittering prizes myself, so I know how easy it is to fall into the trap. The only solution is to work with one program at a time until you have mastered it. 'Committing to your Wealth Creation' also deals with this issue and ensures that you will lock your commitment to fulfilling your desires so deeply into your subconscious, you cannot fail to succeed.

Key Block No 5: Lack of Patience

How cultivating patience is one of the best virtues you can have

We live in a world where everything is faster than it has been since the world began. Technology ensures that we can get answers to any question we might want to ask – instantly. We have fast cars, fast food, and fast communications. As a result, we've grown into a culture of instant gratification seekers. We don't like to have to wait or to persevere to get satisfaction. We want it NOW. In short, we lack patience. But if we can learn to slow down and be patient, we can achieve far more than if we rush headlong towards the next quick fix. The best way to do that is to run an inventory of any projects (personal growth, work related, family related etc.) that you decided you wanted, but gave up for lack of commitment and patience when you didn't see instant results? See how much you shock yourself with this one!

Lack of patience: my advice

Much of what I have said in Key Issue Number 3, 'Expecting Diamonds From Dust: Unrealistic Expectations' can be applied here. Of course you are anxious to start earning money, finding the love of your life, or whatever your dream is, but remember that you have to build up your new mental mind-set and this takes time. You need faith and tenacity in spades. But if you systematically work to your plan, the rewards will come.

Lack of patience: my steepest learning curve

Impatience is my biggest fault in everything. I want everything done yesterday or sooner. However, I realized I needed to work through tasks systematically. I have improved massively with the help of my recordings and I meditate every day. I can't stress enough how important it is to keep playing these recordings as they have enormous impact on your psyche so forgive me for repeating this. Discover the Universal Laws in this System, put them into practice, trust the universe, and be patient. My MP3 'Understanding the Law of Attraction' also addresses this issue and will ensure you have more patience than you've ever had before.

Key Block No 6: Blame Culture

Why removing the blame culture from your mental make-up will give you a sense of freedom like never before.

This is probably the most negative concept I can think of that holds people back – scratch that, it doesn't just hold them back, it puts a massive wall of resistance up in front of them that prevents any good getting in. I was one of those people with a tendency to blame everything and everyone for everything bad that happens to them. When I blamed everything outside of myself in this way, I was denying my own true power and was always focusing on the negative. Through discovering the Laws of the Universe, I came to understand the essential truth that nobody is responsible for what happens in my life but myself. Nobody else is to blame. I am the master of my own fate, regardless of what the external world throws at me. And so are you the master of yours.

I will explain in detail the Law of Attraction shortly, but in brief, it is the principle that what you focus on, you get, so if you happen to be guilty of 'Blame Syndrome' like I was, then you need to step back and examine your thoughts very carefully in light of this; about how your thoughts not only reflect but create your reality. When you constantly blame everyone and everything outside you, you are not taking responsibility for what is happening within you. You are denying that you have any part in what is going on. But you have absolute power to change how you think and perceive the world. It cannot change for you, but you certainly can change the way you see it. And once you do, the sense of liberation is truly life changing. You will never want to blame anyone, anything or any situation ever again.

Blame culture: my advice- don't play the blame game

Read and re-read this book until you fully understand the Universal Laws of Gratitude, Abundance and Attraction and they really sink in. Because when they do, they will completely alter your worldview. Make notes in your journal as you begin to analyze your blame game. You will be shocked at how much you blame things outside yourself. You'll find yourself blaming the traffic, the office, your colleagues, your partner, your kids, the economy, the government, the terrorists, and on and on.

Then, try to go one whole week without blaming something or someone for anything. You will find this extremely hard to do at first, but what is good about the exercise it that it will instantly raise your awareness about your own 'blame game level'... and once it does, you can have a lot of fun getting that level down to zero. Make it a personal challenge and reward yourself with a few words of praise every time you catch yourself in the act of blaming. Immediately stop it when you realize you are doing it, and reframe your perception that one that fits better with your new reality.

When you know that external events/people/things will happen, no matter what you do, and understand that all you can change is your reaction to them, a wonderful thing happens. You realize the futility of blame and accept that whatever 'is', just 'is', and you can move on, directing what would previously have been negative energy into something much more gratifying for yourself.

Blame culture: my steepest learning curve

I am almost ashamed of how guilty I was of blame syndrome. Now, I try to never play the blame game. I am very aware of my role and my responsibility in everything I do today, and I own my part in any outcomes that irritate or frustrate me. My MP3 'Understanding the Law of Gratitude' will help you release any need to blame others.

Key Block No 7: Not Committing to Your Personal Success

From here on we are losing the NOT part of this block. You are going to commit to Your Wealth Creation. Say it out loud, now. 'I am committed to my Wealth Creation.' Repeat this often.

This final section will explain some ways in which you can approach your new found mission, and once you have done that, you will be ready to start work on your subconscious with the aid of my specially constructed MP3s.

I have mentioned above that you need to have faith and tenacity to succeed. And you do. To succeed in reprogramming your subconscious for the success you truly desire, you need one more thing – and that is commitment. Without it, you will get nowhere fast. You need to approach your 'subconscious mindset shift' the same way as you would any new regime. You need to make a plan, you need to nourish it, and you need to devote time to it - every single day. Whilst it is true that you can begin to see great progress as soon as you start this System and in as little as 30 minutes a day, that is the very minimum. I urge you to spend as much time as possible working on your inner transformation. Remember, the more you put into anything, the more you get out of it.

Committing to your personal success: my advice

Commit to learning more... about yourself and the Universal Laws... this commitment should last a lifetime as we never stop learning and there is always something new for you to discover. I have barely scratched the surface here, but I hope what I have presented has given you the tools needed to realize that the world is your oyster and you can have the life of your dreams, if you are prepared to make that commitment.

Committing to your personal success: my steepest learning curve

It won't work if you don't work at it!

It is no use reading this (or any such book) and then forgetting all about it. You have to work the System, and commit to listening to the MP3s every single day, and monitoring your inner dialogue vigilantly. Once I made the decision to commit to changing my life, I made gigantic leaps forward, and so will you. My MP3 'Committing to your Wealth Creation' covers all the critical points to help you achieve this.

CHAPTER 3

Fundamentals of the Universal Laws

Why understanding these laws is your gateway to the life of your dreams

There are hundreds and hundreds of supposed 'laws' applicable or attributable to the universe, depending on whose point of view you believe. I have distilled these laws down to the three that I believe to be the most basic, fundamental laws, onto which everything else can be tacked. Other aspects are important, but for the beginner you need to start here. These are the Laws of Gratitude, Attraction, and Abundance. As you begin your fascinating journey into the wonderful world of these laws, it is not necessary to worry about any other laws for now. Below, I'll cover these three basic but very powerful universal forces in a simple, easy to follow format that will enable you to begin working with them to improve your life immediately.

Understanding the Law of Gratitude

Why this most profound law will both stun you and change your world-view

The Law of Gratitude is simple yet profound. Countless books have been written on it, and it is a huge subject. But it's not that complicated. Here, I have simplified it so that you can get to the crux very quickly: we need to be grateful for everything that we already have in life. Right here. Right now. No matter how bad your situation might seem, there are always people worse off than you are. Let me ask you a few questions, to demonstrate the point:

- Are you healthy?
- Do you have a roof over your head?
- Do you have food on the table?
- Do you have a job?

If you answer 'Yes' to these questions, then you are already rich beyond the means of 46.9 million people in the United States alone who were officially classed as living in poverty as recently as 2010. It is hard to believe that 17.2 million households did not have enough food to eat. Yet it is true.

Almost half of the world – over three billion people – live on less than $2.50 per day. Can you afford a cup of coffee at Starbucks? If you can you are seriously wealthy compared to these three billion people. Does that not make you think?

Ok, so let's look at some other gifts to be grateful for. Let me ask you a few more questions:

- Do you have electricity?
- Running water?
- Family who love you?
- Friends?

- Places to go out to enjoy eating, exercising, socializing?
- Nice clothes, shoes, cosmetics, jewelry?
- A computer? An i-Pad? Mobile phone?
- A car?

And what about the 2006 study, which pointed out a surprising statistic: "To be among the richest 10% of adults in the world required $61,000 in assets and more than $500,000 was needed to belong to the richest 1% - a group which – with 37 million members worldwide – is far from an exclusive club." A more recent report (2015) put the figures at $68,000 and $759,000 to be in the 10% and 1% categories.

So you only need to have assets of $68,000 to be among the top 10% of the world's richest people. Now I bet you didn't know that - I didn't! So even if you have 50% less than that, you are still probably in the top 20% or 30% of the world's richest people.

But okay, I understand that you'd like to be a lot richer; however, expressing gratitude is the first and most important of the Universal Laws. By constantly being genuinely grateful for all that you have in your life, right here, right now, you are sending out a powerful message to the universe. This message acknowledges your gratitude to the higher realms and positions you to receive more of the same, or better, in your life.

When you sincerely express gratitude you are vibrating at a higher level, one that is in harmony with the universe. Everything is made up of energy; billions of tiny atoms that are vibrating at different speeds. This is scientific fact as I mentioned earlier. What's more important still is that your thoughts are energy, and by sending positive thoughts out to the universe, accompanied by genuine good feelings, you are in charge of what you manifest. It is that simple.

Wealthy people give generously because they can and because they are driven by a passion far greater than the desire to acquire money for money's sake. Let me share a few examples and quotes here with you, just to illustrate my point:

- In 2012, Warren Buffet pledged $3 billion to charitable foundations run by his children.
- Bill Gates has already given over $28 billion to charity, in addition to now pledging the rest of his $58 billion fortune to causes he believes in.
- Mark Zukerburg (the founder of Facebook) donated $498.8 million in stock to Silicon Valley Community Foundation. Mark Zuckerberg has often said that money was of no interest to him. It seems that quite often, those who do not desperately chase down money but chase their dream instead, have money flowing back to them by the truckload.
- Music mogul Simon Cowell, who regularly donates to children and animal charities, told Esquire magazine that he will leave his £220+ million fortune to 'kids and dogs'. He does not believe in passing money from generation to generation (including his own son) and

believes people need to make their own success in life. Cowell plans to work until he's 80 or 90. Clearly, money is not what drives him.

- Nor does it drive the charismatic and fabulously wealthy Oprah Winfrey, who has given more than $41 million through her Charity Foundation.

Some Famous Quotes from the Super-Wealthy

"Is the rich world aware of how four billion of the six billion live? If we were aware, we would want to help out, we'd want to get involved."

Bill Gates

"Facebook was not originally created to be a company. It was built to accomplish a social mission – to make the world more open and connected"

Mark Zuckerberg

"Your legacy has to be that hopefully you gave enough people an opportunity, so that they could do well, and you gave them your time, taught them what you know."

Simon Cowell

"Be thankful for what you have; you will end up having more.

If you concentrate on what you do not have, you will never, ever have enough"

Oprah Winfrey

"Gratitude is the healthiest of all human emotions. The more you express gratitude for what you have, the more likely you will have even more to express gratitude for."

Zig Ziglar

"It is through gratitude for the present moment that the spiritual dimension of life opens up."

Eckhart Tolle

Why The Power Of Emotion Matters To Gratitude

Probably the most critical component of changing your world from the inside out resides exactly there… within, where the 'real you' exists. No matter how much outward work you might do, unless you align your vibrational frequency with the true, genuine emotions of the success you want to achieve, you will probably fail. This is absolutely crucial for you to understand. You MUST attach strong feelings of genuine, happy emotion to your thoughts. You can't just pay lip service, and here's another irrefutable fact you need to know – you can't fool the universe. It won't work if you take a lackadaisical attitude like 'Yeah yeah, sure I am grateful...' You MUST really feel it and believe that you are indeed a very lucky person to have all you have in your life, right here, right now. The power of emotion is going to play a huge part in your success, so get used to tuning into the right vibrational frequency. I'll show you how to do that in The 6 Fundamental Steps To Your Success: Shortcut Secrets later in this book.

My special MP3 accompanying this System will teach you how to fully express gratitude for everything in your life and in everything you do each day. It is the cornerstone, the very foundation of your journey to creating the life of your dreams.

I could add dozens more pages about how the wealthy think and how much they give and enjoy giving, but you are starting to see the point. The principle of gratitude is always evident in giving back. The more people give, the more they seem to get back themselves.

Of course, I hear you say, these people can afford to give this kind of money away without it compromising their luxurious lifestyles. And that is absolutely true. But if they can generate such wealth and benefit the less fortunate to such tremendous degrees as a result, don't they deserve all the luxury they have and desire? I think they do.

Understanding the Law of Attraction

Why knowing how this law works can be your gateway to wealth and happiness

The Law of Attraction simply stated means that 'like attracts like' and 'what you think about, you become' or, 'what you focus on, you get'. This has been written in hundreds of different ways, but the crux of it remains the same. The message was written in the Bible, and was known to ancient sages long before the Bible was written, so it has been around for a very long time.

What is most interesting about this quote on the right however is that we are known to 'think' with our minds. By stating 'he' (you) thinketh with 'his' (your) heart, the message is clear: it is your emotions, your feelings – as I mentioned above - that truly speak to you. Not your mind, not your brain. You talk about being 'heartbroken' or having a 'heart overflowing with love'... you do not say 'I was mind broken' or 'My mind is overflowing with love'. You always ascribe your feelings to your heart.

In his classic essay, 'As a Man Thinketh', James Allen puts it like this:

"The aphorism, "As a man thinketh in his heart so is he," not only embraces the whole of a man's being, but is so comprehensive as to reach out to every condition and circumstance of his life. A man is literally what he thinks, his character being the complete sum of all his thoughts."

Japanese researcher and alternative healer Dr Masaru Emoto carried out some fascinating experiments on how the power of thought affects water and the subsequent crystal formations. Water that was given thoughts of love produced stunning snowflake crystals of immense beauty. Those given thoughts of hate produced ugly, malformed crystals. If thought can do this to water, imagine what it can do for you. The pictures below are from Dr Emoto's wonderful book, 'The Hidden Messages in Water' and is one I highly recommend you read.

The Photo on the left is of an ice crystal frozen from severely polluted water. The photo on the right is the same water re-frozen after having been blessed by Dr Emoto. One can plainly see that we do have the ability to not only heal ourselves, but our Earth as well.

There can be no doubt about it – your thoughts create your reality and your feelings. I have read literally hundreds of books on the Law of Attraction, downloaded dozens of programs, PDFs, MP3s, videos and courses and the majority of them tell you this irrefutable fact. If you want your life to change, then start right now by filling your days with thoughts of gratitude, love, happiness, kindness, success; align your vibrational frequency with emotions and feelings that fill you with the truth of these as reality in your life - and wealth and happiness will surely follow.

These are but a minuscule sample of a universal truth that has been written and talked about for centuries. You are what you think you are, and what you think about influences your feelings and your reality. That is it, in a nutshell. If you have read the book 'The Secret' by Rhonda Byrne, you might have felt a little disillusioned, as I did, when the 'miracles' didn't start to happen right away. That was back in 2006 and I still had quite a lot of Law of Attraction reading to catch up on at that point!

The fact is, whilst it is a wonderful book, some critical components were missing from The Secret. Some of the stars of the subsequent film admitted as much.

The Power of Intention and The Law of Attraction

All you need to do to get the laws working for you in a positive way is set a clear intention about what you want, and tell the universe. Basically the Law of Attraction is working for everyone, by reflecting back to them what they think about most. So if you are constantly worrying about money, relationships, and feeling down because of all your problems, that is what the universe is picking up on, and giving you back more of. Your vibrational frequency is negative. If you have read Law of Attraction by Abraham-Hicks, you will already be very familiar with this concept. Your feelings and emotions are negative. So, you are surely going to get back more of the same. You can change that by putting out thoughts of what you do want in life with feelings attached, as I mentioned above. So set a great intention for what you do want and fill it with the powerful emotions of how you will feel when you do get it.

You can write this down and read it every single day. Be specific. Do not say 'I want to be rich' – put an amount on it that signifies richness to you. If you are looking for your ideal partner, describe him or her, outline the key qualities that you are seeking in that person. If you want to lose weight or get fit, be specific in what those goals are and affirm that you will achieve them. Then ask the universe to go to work on your dreams, and then, most importantly, let it go with a feeling of trust... do not keep doubting the universe or asking for the same thing over and over again. If you do this, it's like saying 'I trust you but just in case... here's my request again' – meaning, you do NOT really trust the process. You must believe and trust in the process for it to work. Then take inspired action to make your dreams a reality. Following this System will give you everything you need to take that inspired action, whilst the MP3 recordings will hammer these points deep into your subconscious; you have got absolutely everything you need here to succeed.

Understanding the power of these exercises is vitally important, as you will need to draw on them when you begin your 'Creative Visualization' work. So get into the habit of calling up those good feelings as often as you can and attach them to your intentions, dozens of times a day. But just to clarify that I am not contradicting what I have said above about trust. What I am talking about here is having the feelings of abundance, of having what it is you want, as often as you can because this raises your vibrational frequency, regardless of whether all the goodies have arrived yet. The more good feelings you have, the more of the same you will attract into your life – focus on what you do want to manifest in your life - that's written in stone according to the Law of Attraction. You might find it helpful to make a vision board with images that instantly bring to mind feelings of happiness to you. You can do this really easily by using www.pinterest.com. Set up your free account, and type in whatever symbolizes your dreams/desires. You will find everything you could possibly imagine in there! Do whatever it takes to make yourself feel good. More on this later!

Understanding the Law of Abundance

Why understanding this law can literally change your entire perception of wealth and who deserves it

There is more than enough of everything to go around. You might find that hard to believe, as I did when I first came across this notion. But it is a fact. It is the distribution of everything that is the issue. Some people have far too much, or so it would often seem, and others have far too little. If you think there is not enough food in the world – and as I have mentioned, there are plenty of starving people on the planet – think again. It is not because of a lack of food. It is due to a number of other factors.

A report in the UK's Daily Mail in March 2012 reported the shocking headline:

"Up to 50% of the world's food goes to waste as the average American throws away 400lbs. of food each year."

They included the graph shown below, to illustrate this startling reality.

Municipal Solid Waste Discarded (by material) in 2010

Y-axis: Million / tons (0 to 40)

X-axis: Materials

- Food Waste: 33.79
- Plastics: 28.49
- Paper and Paperboard: 26.74
- Metals: 14.54
- Wood: 13.58
- Yard Waste: 14.2
- Textiles: 11.15
- Glass: 8.4
- Rubber and Leather: 6.61
- Other: 3.38

In 2010 alone, more than 34 millions tons of food waste was generated in the United States, as this graph shows

And in the UK, it's equally bad as around 15 million tonnes of food is thrown away every year – 50% of which comes from domestic households.

According to the United Nations Environment Programme, (UNEP) roughly a third of all food produced annually – 1.3 billion tonnes – is wasted. Whilst the reasons are many and complex, one thing should be clear, there is an abundance of food. If we take this one step further, consider how many people are overweight or clinically obese: fast food chains and restaurants present diners with portions far in excess of dietary needs, and people get used to eating more than they need because it seems normal. Obesity in the US has reached epidemic proportions and in 2014 was reported that nearly two-thirds of the UK's population were obese.

And here's an excellent example of where all the excess food has gone to fat, from an article entitled 'Just How Fat Are We?' by Ellen Fanning in The Global Mail, June 2013:

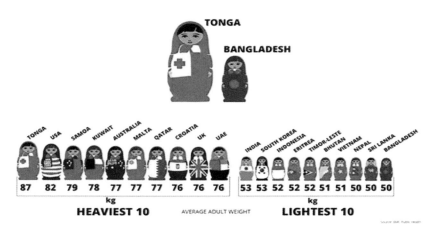

Note: Links to the graphs/research cited here can be found at the end of this chapter.

When you stop and think about these types of statistics, your perspective starts to shift, doesn't it? Mine did!

However, back to wealth and abundance. What is important to understand is that wealth is relative. Let's say you are a young man in Africa. Some anonymous benefactor sends a sparkling new red Ferrari to your little village. What good would the Ferrari be to you? Your idea of wealth and riches would require delivery of completely different goods.

What we value or consider as wealth varies greatly depending on where we live, our cultural backgrounds, our country's politics and so on. I am not saying that those living in less 'fortunate' circumstances than you do not deserve your compassion and indeed, your support, as often as you can give it. Even if you have a low income, you can volunteer your time, or help a friend or a stranger in need. Give If you can because the universe loves giving and generosity as much as it loves gratitude and you will get it back a hundredfold because giving in any form sends out a great message of thanks and gratitude to the universe. You know the saying... what goes around, comes around... it is true.

But even within our own cultures, our values can differ markedly in our definition of what wealth is, or what wealth means to us. I know people who believe that owning an Aston Martin would fulfil their dreams. Others see a gold Rolex as the ultimate status symbol. Personally, if I were to win either one, I would sell them right away, as cars and watches, no matter what they cost, just do not signify 'wealth' to me in the way they do to someone else.

For me, a reasonably good standard of living, a nice home and financial freedom are important, but being able to give generously means a lot more to me than owning an Aston Martin. I am not saying this to make you think I am some kind of saint... I'm no saint. I found that for me, when I reached a place in my life where I had plenty of everything I needed, the greatest pleasures I got were from being able to treat my family to things they were not able to afford and to be able to donate to causes that mean a lot to me personally.

Not that there's anything wrong with wanting gorgeous, glamorous, shiny things – I have a huge collection of Swarovski jewelry because I just LOVE sparkly things! It is all down to personal priorities and taste. We are all different; therefore what makes us happy materially will be different too. I might hire a yacht for a month and take my family and friends around the Caribbean but I'd never in a million years want to buy one, even if I could afford a fleet of them. However YOU might.

But before you can go get your Aston Martin, Rolex or whatever it is that 'floats your boat', you must understand that wealth is a concept you need to be comfortable with. Many people, although they 'wish' to win the lottery or be left a vast fortune by some distant relative they'd forgotten all about, would in fact be very uncomfortable with the money should it suddenly manifest itself. I remember one time a Euro Millions Lottery of £161 million was up for grabs. I was in the UK at the time, and everyone had bought tickets and was talking about it. Yet on contemplation of what they would do if they actually had the winning numbers, I lost count of the people who said "It's too much money!" and accompanied the comment with slumped shoulders or looks of despair on their faces at the prospect.

For some people, wealth like this is income-prehensible. My world-view was very different. If I won that amount of money, the 1.6 billion US Mega jackpot (the highest so far in US lottery history at the time of writing), my first thought would be: 'Wow, now I can really do some good and change a lot of people's lives for the better.' When I explained this to people, it still took a while for them to realize that you do not have to keep all that money. You could distribute it among family and friends and make hundreds of people individual millionaires. Or you could divide it up between yourself, your family, and still give multi-millions to your favorite charities. Or you could set up your own foundation for a cause you support and believe in. There's no limit to what you could do with that kind of money.

What is vital to understand about money is that its real currency is energy. Money is just paper. It is what you can do with it that matters, and having a very clear vision about what that is for you is really important. Being poor doesn't help anyone to help anyone else. So the more wealth you can attract into your life, the more you can help others along the way and I know from personal experience, giving to people, whether it is a family member or a stranger in the street, makes you feel great!

Wealth – An Alternative Definition

Wealth is not necessarily about money. There are many wealthy people who are not happy. True, most of us would rather be rich and unhappy than poor and unhappy.... but money is not the only driving force in life that has great importance for us. There are several categories where you can consider 'wealth' aside from financial: emotional, physical, spiritual, career, relationships. Maybe you are financially free but emotionally deadlocked? In a destructive or negative relationship? Lonely? Shy? Maybe you are afraid you'll never meet the love of your life, your soul mate? Maybe you have a great income but hate your job? All of these issues can be resolved if you apply the techniques in this System to your thinking, no matter what area of your life you want to improve. Put your thoughts under the microscope, question them, examine them, and determine what it is you want instead of what you are getting. Then set about changing your thought patterns and you will start to manifest the things you truly do desire in life, be it wealth, health, love, or abundance in whatever form is significant for you.

The 6 Fundamental Steps to Your Success: Shortcut Secrets

These simple steps can galvanize your efforts to attract the life of your dreams

The method is really quite simple and I can put it into six steps that I believe to be the fundamental principles of success; they have worked for me, and they will work for you.

1. Understand how the Universal Laws work and be open minded about them.
2. Clear your self-limiting beliefs.
3. Practice gratitude often, every day.

4. Focus on feeling good and projecting those good feelings into yourself and your surroundings as much as you possibly can as you visualize the future you desire.
5. Set your intention, plan your dream, and take inspired action that makes you feel good.
6. Keep learning & listening to motivational books, videos, recordings, webinars and seminars – particularly those that come with this system, until you really know that you've 'got it' - until you can feel the seismic shift. This is important because as you evolve and assimilate new information, it is vital to keep both your conscious and subconscious minds focused in the right direction - and you do that by constantly 'feeding' it more powerful, positive, motivational material. This includes getting into meditation, which I've also covered in this book.

Can you feel good instantly? How to change Your Vibrational Resonance

3 fantastic techniques to eliminate negative thoughts and change your mood in minutes

Sometimes, when you feel really low, it can be very hard to change your emotional state but it can be done, and here I want to share 3 techniques with you to try next time you are struggling and feeling down. These techniques can be incredibly effective so do give them all a try to find the one that works best for you. And make sure to use it any time you start to feel low and note how easily you have changed your vibrational frequency!

Technique No. 1: Using memory based affirmative cues

Read these instructions first. Then, sit and relax, take a few deep breaths. Close your eyes.

Allow your mind to drift back to a sad or traumatic situation in your life. Just bring the thought/picture/feeling into your awareness for a few moments. Let the feelings associated with the memory come to the surface. Notice how you feel. Sad? Down? Depressed? I am pretty sure you feel miserable right now. Sorry! So let's change that now.

When you open your eyes, shake your head to clear it. Next, take a few more deep breaths. Sit back, relax, and close your eyes. Now allow your mind to go back to the most joyful moment in your life, for example:

- Your wedding day
- The birth of your first child
- Passing your driving test
- Getting a great score in your exams
- Your first love
- Getting a promotion at work
- Making a brilliant sale

- Having a fantastic idea that turned out to be a winner
- Any other event that filled you with happiness

Bring the picture/feelings/thoughts associated with that event into sharp focus in your mind. Let those wonderful memories come flooding to the surface. Remember the sounds, the smells. What you were wearing? Above all, remember how you felt. Feelings are the language the universe understands. Savour those feelings for a few moments, and then open your eyes. Notice how you feel now. I bet there is a BIG difference. Do you understand now how easily you can shift your vibrational resonance into one of happiness and joy? This is absolutely key. The more you can keep yourself in this happy state, the better, so get used to practicing this a lot, every day, even for a few minutes. Call to mind the happy times and really let those feelings wash over you. And do this every day. Bring those gorgeous feelings back. The more you do this, the easier it will be to shift your mind-set into the vibrational resonance that you want. And thus, you will attract more of the same.

Technique No. 2: Using activity based affirmative cues

This is even simpler to carry out. When you feel down, do the above only this time, instead of calling up happy memories, let your mind drift into activities that you love doing on a regular basis. These should be activities that bring you happiness, joy or great pleasure. Dancing, playing sport, singing, playing your guitar, listening to music (one of my tops!), playing with your dog (another of my tops!), having a fun day out with your children, a romantic dinner with your partner, making love… whatever works for you. Think about it and feel the emotions… and keep them with you as long as you can. Do this exercise often – it only takes a few minutes and will instantly shift your mood.

Technique No. 3: Negativity analysis

Sometimes, despite your best intentions, the above techniques may not get the job done. That is when you need to dig deeper, and do something different. So if this applies to you, you need to revisit your self-limiting beliefs techniques and ask yourself some questions.

Why are you feeling this way now? Is it reactive or organic? If it is a reaction to a person or situation, say it or write it down. Express exactly what you are feeling and why. Jotting it down also helps to remove it to a degree, and as you are going to jot down a lot of thoughts from now on, it is a good idea to do this anytime you feel negative. It will help you identify any patterns and highlight areas you could work on more deeply during the System. If it is organic, then you need to keep asking yourself questions until the answers come. There is a reason hidden underneath the emotion. You need to find it.

Once you have got a clear analysis of why you are feeling this, you are ready to move on to the next part.

Face the negative emotion head on. How does it feel? If you could describe it, how would it look? For me, when I get a serious 'down' moment, it feels like a heavy brown lump in my solar plexus. It is important to acknowledge the emotion.

How does it rate on a scale of 1-10? Give it a ranking on your negativity scale.

Ask yourself what the lesson is here for you? What is the negative emotion trying to tell you? If you think of it as being opposite to what you do want, that makes it easier to identify what the lesson might be. You can learn from the situation. An example could be that you are angry with a colleague who took the credit for a job you had done all the work for. You are furious at your colleague. You leave work in a bad mood, and feel progressively worse as the day goes on, until you are seething with anger and resentment. Some of the questions you might ask yourself then are: 'Why did I not speak up? Why did I not take the colleague aside and explain how I felt? How could this have happened to me? Why is life so unfair?' Now, ask yourself what you feel about this. You might start thinking: 'I am too weak to stand up for myself' or 'I do not believe in myself' or 'I am not good enough' or thoughts along those lines. There will be underlying reasons. You need to dig to find them. Go into the emotion as much as you can. Really get to know it. What has it told you? What have you learned from it?

Once you have identified the reasons take several deep breaths, right into the area of anguish. Imagine you could draw in a clean shining white light into your body. Look up as you breathe out. Looking up has an immense physiological impact that reflects immediately on your psyche – it is hard to feel down when you 'look up', (as the saying implies). Looking up is uplifting. As you breathe out, imagine that you are letting all than anguish out of your body. Do this several times.

This exercise is extremely powerful in helping you understand the deeper workings of your mind. Usually this exercise is enough to rid you of the negative feelings altogether. Check to see how you rate your feelings now? If any residual negativity remains, tell yourself that this is just a situation, it is temporary, it is not who you ARE. It will not last and that is an absolute certainty. Then repeat the process again until it is gone.

Practice these 3 key techniques every time you feel down in any way. You will be surprised at how quickly you can shift your internal state and by doing this, you are raising your vibrational resonance or energy to a higher frequency, and this is what the universe needs from you. Positive vibrations galore!

Some final thoughts

Having money to adequately provide for yourself and your loved ones is something that the universe fully supports you with. You may feel sympathetic to people less fortunate than you, in your own and other countries, and having plenty money flowing in and out of your life will give you the means to help, so go out and grab it with both hands. The universe wants you to have everything you desire, and if you practice the advice given in this book, and listen to the MP3 recordings every day, you will begin to see incredible changes in your life.

And I will stress one more time – you must be prepared to practice, practice, practice, and commit to your new way of thinking. All the successful people who work the Law of Attraction will tell you this. Do not just read this book, have a half-hearted listen to the MP3s and give up when you do not see instant results. The Law of Attraction does take time. Remember patience? You need patience and you need to practice and you need to believe that success will come to you. And it surely will.

Remember that what you give out, in your thoughts and actions, you get back. Applying these principles in your own life, with a genuine and generous spirit, will send the most powerful message imaginable to the universe. And it will work for you, no matter who you are, where you are, or what your current situation. Believe that you deserve everything the universe has to offer, if you have the will to achieve it. The universe does not discriminate on that point. If you are willing to be open, to do the extra work suggested in this

System, then without a shadow of a doubt, you have the means to achieve great abundance!

Ask yourself this question, and be totally honest in your response: up until now have you achieved everything you desire using the methods you have always adopted? If the answer to this question is NO, then surely you owe it to yourself to try a new approach? That new approach lies within the contents of this System. If you follow it with commitment, your life will change for the better in ways you never imagined possible.

Who am I and why should you listen to me?

In case you are interested, here's a bit about my story.

At this point, before I get into the elements of the actual recordings and how you should use them, I thought you might like to know a little bit about me, and how I came to create Cogni-Fusion Mind Expansion Technology. Of course if you're not interested I don't mind at all if you skip this and head straight to the best part – Chapter Four.

My Background

I'd had some very tough times until I got the Law of Attraction working for me again. In the early '90's I was practicing Hypnotherapy and NLP in my clinic in London's Covent Garden, as well as doing voluntary work for an organization supporting substance misusers with HIV in Brixton. These were challenging and rewarding times. However, international travel beckoned and I moved to Hong Kong. That was the beginning of 18 years of travelling and working in the UAE, setting up my own recruitment business, which then failed miserably due to the economic downturn. However, by understanding and working the Law of Attraction, I manifested not one but two brilliant, high paying jobs. One was in Abu Dhabi, and one in Azerbaijan. When my contract ended in Azerbaijan, I returned to the UAE. Much as I loved my work in HR, the Law of Attraction was starting to play a much more important role in my life than I realized.

My Dilemma

I was now a six-figure salary earner. I knew that if I wanted to continue with this profession, I could easily have done so. I already had an interview lined up for a major oil company in Qatar. But, I asked myself, 'Is this what I want to do for the rest of my life?' And at this point I could feel a mental shift taking place. A life-changing shift. I knew that the changes I'd experienced in my life had not been down to pure luck, but to applying the principles of the Law of Attraction. It was powerful and I knew it. And if the Law of Attraction had worked so well for me, then surely it could work just as well for anyone else.

My Decision

By now I had been studying the Law of Attraction for some time and listening to a lot of MP3s on the subject when suddenly the lessons I had learned leapt out and became very clear to me. I felt a very strong intuitive pull to return to the field of therapy and personal growth. I am a huge fan of personal development and had kept practicing Hypnotherapy, Reiki and Emotional Freedom Technique (EFT) over the years with family and friends. Suddenly and without any shred of doubt, I knew what I had to do. It was the proverbial 'light bulb' moment. I decided to continue studying and developing my knowledge of personal growth and therapy, fields that resonate with me on every level and which I am deeply passionate about.

My Therapy Breakthrough

I began studying with the enthusiasm that can only spring from a deeply intense passion. I had found my true calling in life. During my research I came across Brainwave Entrainment and music based therapy to effect rapid personal change in people's lives. This turned out to be a very exciting time for me. I have always found music to be a great mood enhancer, and had used music for my therapy sessions previously. After further research, I found some incredible software that allowed me to make my own subliminal recordings using Brainwave Entrainment. I was thrilled to have found it! I began experimenting with various techniques, adding

Hypnotherapy, NLP, and Subliminal Suggestions to the mix, and used myself as my first guinea pig.

The success I immediately experienced with the biggest bane of my life - weight loss - was utterly astonishing. I could not believe how something I had struggled with for years suddenly changed, literally overnight, as a result of making myself a subliminal recording. In the following few months I dropped 20 lbs. Not only did I lose weight, but also I cured my insomnia – something I had lived with for years!

I started making recordings for my family and friends, and they proved so effective I simply knew I had to return to the world of therapy full time – but this time, I wanted to focus on having an online business due to the extensive reach and incredible freedom it allows. So I set about changing my career. I upgraded all my skills and qualified as a Master Life Coach.

Another light-bulb moment

By combining the power of the Laws of the Universe with my system to deliver them straight to your subconscious, I had created a winning formula. I discovered that people struggle with definite blocks that get in the way of their success. The next 'Light Bulb Moment' occurred when I realized that by combining the two methods, I could put together highly effective Systems that would help people to realize results fast and I created the 'Cogni-Fusion' Mind Expansion Technology method I have explained in this book, and this System is the result. You are going to experience this incredible technology for yourself when you download all the Cogni-Fusion MP3s that come with this book.

The Law of Attraction grabbed me and has held me in its thrall to the point that I am pretty obsessed with it because I have seen what it can do once you understand it. This System will show you how to make it work for you.

This is No 1 in the Cogni-Fusion Personal Development Series and I will be adding 2 or 3 new titles this year, with the aim of publishing 10 titles in due course. I want to achieve my big dream of helping thousands of people to 'Change Their World From the Inside Out', with Cogni-Fusion Mind Expansion Technology. By doing this course, you are helping me achieve my dream too and I am sincerely thankful and grateful to you for your purchase. I will be sending out my thoughts of gratitude to you and the Universe for your health, wealth and abundance.

Get in Touch with me...

I would be very happy to hear of your journey and your progress. I would greatly value your feedback and comments on this Program so please feel free to email me at any time. I have created a special email especially for you so that your email will not get lost amongst all my other incoming!

Email: mailto:mariaprivatemembers@gmail.com

Website: http://www.mariamcmahon.com

You can also find me on my Facebook page:

https://www.facebook.com/mariamcmahoncognifusion/

And of course if you could leave even a short review and rating on Amazon, goodreads or your favorite book website, I would be immensely grateful to you. And of course, connect with me in goodreads if you are a regular in there.

I wish you joy on your journey to Changing Your World From The Inside Out!

PS: The Fedex Logo…

I didn't forget. It's very clear that it's just FedEx isn't it? But if you look at the white space between the 'E' and 'x' in 'Ex', you will spot a white arrow pointing to the right. It's a crafty (subliminal) way of implying speed and forward movement! Go back and have a look now and you will be amazed at how obvious it is.

Please continue now to Chapter 4 for the full Product Information and Instructions.

CHAPTER 4

How to Use The Law of Attraction Shortcut Secrets Cogni-Fusion Mind Expansion Technology MP3s

To access all the downloads, go to the link below to register if you have exhibited extreme self-control and not done so yet!

http://www.mariamcmahon.com/membership-signup/

This System brings you five incredibly powerful MP3s that have been specifically designed and recorded to accompany this book. Each MP3 will embed the lessons learned in the book firmly and deeply into your subconscious mind. In addition to that, I have included TWO versions of the MP3s... the full 60-minute versions and shorter 30-minute versions. I have also added, as a special bonus, The Powerhouse Five, and 2 more bonus MP3s, all detailed below. So you will have plenty to keep you going for quite some time!

Each MP3 in this System has been compiled using between six to eight layers of carefully constructed recordings, with the best technology available, to deliver the most powerful effect to both your conscious and subconscious mind. It is advisable to use headphones when listening to the recordings to get the best effect. Each recording is 60 minutes in duration.

All Cogni-Fusion MP3s in this System are unique. I use a variety of inductions and therapeutic techniques that may seem simple but are all designed with a specific purpose in mind: to help you reach effective change as quickly as possible. When recordings are layered in the way I do them, much of what is going on bypasses your conscious mind and enters the subconscious, where effective change takes place. All subliminal messages are recorded either by 'real' people or myself - they are not the computer-generated text-to-speech recordings that come with some programs.

IMPORTANT NOTE: Whilst all the recordings are 60 minutes, you can elect to listen to the short, 30-minute versions if you are short of time after you have initially listened to them fully the first time. The subliminal messages start about 10 minutes into the recordings and run through to the end so no matter how long you listen, you will reap the benefits.

How to use this System

Basically, it's quite straightforward. Do the exercise to determine your self-limiting beliefs - make sure you write them down, and start with the first MP3, then work your way through 2,3,4 & 5. If you have never done any creative visualization, I recommend you play the Creative Visualization

- Nature Trail MP3 Bonus track after MP3 1, and before you move on to the rest. This will help you visualize much more easily as you work through 2,3,4 & 5. However, I'd like to provide you with a step-by-step process, so here goes!

Preparation for Listening To The Recordings

When you first play the 5 recordings in this System, please set aside the full 60 minutes to allow yourself to thoroughly clear all blocks and fully absorb the messages in each one. The recordings are designed to reinforce everything you learn as you go along.

Set aside time to relax when you will not be disturbed. Turn off your phone. Settle down in a nice comfy chair, or on your bed (prior to sleep is always a good time to listen).

Whilst Isochronic Tones can be listened to without headphones, for a more personal and dynamic experience, I recommend headphones/ear buds for all recordings (unless specifically for daytime listening and then they are optional).

And one more important thing… do not worry if you cannot make out everything that is being said, and do not consciously try to follow everything that is going on – you can't, there is too much! This is why the recordings are so effective. They force you to 'give up and give in'… the key is to relax, let go, and let your subconscious do the work. It is more than capable!

This is where your real journey to reprogramming your mind begins. Do not dilute the effects by giving the System less than your full commitment.

CAUTION: SAFETY NOTICE

You should NEVER listen to these recordings whilst driving or operating machinery, or doing anything that requires focused concentration, with the exception of the Powerhouse Five Bonus MP3, which can be listened to during the day. All of these recordings have Isochronic Tones Brainwave Entrainment which is safe for anyone to listen to, **but if you have suffered with epilepsy, are taking psychotropic drugs, are pregnant or use a pacemaker, you should consult your physician before listening to this program.**

Here is the step-by-step process:

1.   Read this book and absorb its contents. Re-read it as often as you need to before starting the Program, so that you are fully confident in the process.

2.   Review the notes you made as you as you read through the book, because you will need to identify your self-limiting beliefs. This should take no more than a week.

3.   When you are clear about those, listen to Cogni-Fusion MP3 1 'Blast Your Self-Limiting Beliefs' every day until you feel certain that you have eliminated all your negative beliefs. This can happen in one session for some people, others may need to play it several times. Only you can know for sure. Also note that you may eliminate several beliefs, but subsequently through your own learning and development, realize that you have identified new limiting beliefs. In this case, you can always return to this MP3 to blast those away too. Once you have done the above, you are now ready to start laying down new programming to your subconscious mind.

4.   Play the next Cogni-Fusion MP3 2 'Understanding the Law of Gratitude' for 7 days. Notice how you begin to feel more gratitude in your everyday life. You will find yourself looking for more and more to be grateful for.

5.   Next, move on to MP3 3 'Understanding the Law of Attraction' for 7 days. Notice how your thinking begins to change.

6.   Next, move on to MP3 4 'Understanding the Law of Abundance 7 days. Again, notice how your thinking begins to change.

7.   Next, move on to MP3 5: 'Committing to Your Wealth Creation' for 7 days. Notice that you now feel an inner resolve that you did not feel before.

8.   Next, start playing the 'Law of Attraction Shortcut Secrets Powerhouse' every day during work. You can play this as long as you care to, but definitely for 7 days initially. If your working environment does not permit you to listen then make sure to listen to it at home or wherever you can.

9.   In the evening, choose one of the three bonus MP3s to listen to. Alternate which bonus MP3 you listen to each evening.

10.   Continue with this System for 90 days, rotating the MP3s or choosing to listen to the ones you feel you need to more often. During this time be vigilant about your thoughts. If you find yourself thinking, feeling or saying anything negative, make a note of it, and go back to MP3 1 and run through that again to eliminate those negative beliefs. You can also return to the 'Top 10 Category' section at any time to shed further light on any new issues that come up.

11.   Remember the Power of Feelings and Intention, so that every time you set an intention you fuel it up by tuning into the feelings of happiness, joy, and prosperity that you want to attain. Keep your

vibrational resonance at the frequency that will ensure the universe sends back more of the same to you.

After 90 days you will see and feel a big difference in your life and you will want to continue feeding your subconscious with more of these life-changing programs. I cannot stress enough how important it is to keep listening to these recordings on a daily basis. It is essential to keep feeding your subconscious with these new positive and affirmative programs.

If you stop, there is always the danger that you will revert to your old habits, and believe me, I have been guilty of this too. Now, there is not a day goes by that I do not 'feed' my brain! I spend 20 or 30 minutes in the evening meditating, I spend the last hour or so every day reading books on my Kindle – almost always on Law of Attraction, Brain Science, Spirituality, and finally, I go to sleep listening to one of my BWE subliminal MP3s. I love them because I know how powerful they are! And you will too, once you realize the power of your incredible subconscious mind.

Breakdown of the Law of Attraction Shortcut Secrets Cogni-Fusion Mind Expansion Technology System

In this section, I'm going to share with you some specific details of what each Cogni-Fusion MP3 is designed to facilitate. All of these recordings contain a number of layers, combining relaxation, hypnotherapy inductions, suggestions, deepeners, Brainwave Entrainment, music, nature, nature, music, NLP (on some of them), subliminal messages, and a variety of my signature Cogni-Fusion Mind Expansion Technology effects.

MP3 1: Blast Your Self-limiting Beliefs

Cogni-Fusion 8 Layer Session: This MP3s deals with 1 and 2 of the 7 Key Issues that are blocking your progress: Self-Limiting Beliefs and Self-Sabotage.

This is the start of your incredible journey to the life of your dreams. This complex 8-layer Cogni-Fusion recording is carefully constructed to take you into a deeply relaxed state, wherein you will be taken through the process of releasing your self-limiting beliefs. The Cogni-Fusion Techniques will enable you to eradicate your current belief system that is preventing you from succeeding. This recoding will truly set you free from everything that is holding you back.

The type of layering I use in these recordings ensures that both your conscious and sub-conscious mind have plenty to absorb. It is also great if you are overly analytical as the technique allows much of the content to bypass your conscious facility.

Some examples of the Subliminal Suggestions on this recording are:

I let go of all self-limiting beliefs

I choose to be positive

I let go of anything that no longer serves me

MP3 2: Understanding the Law of Gratitude

Cogni-Fusion 7 Layer Session: This MP3 deals with Key Issue No. 6: Blame Culture.

When you put yourself into a position of gratitude, and really feel that gratitude for all the great gifts you already have in your life, a wonderful thing happens... you begin to lose the desire to blame other people. Because you have a new understanding of the universal laws, your perspective will shift exponentially. This 7-layer recording will reinforce the Law of Gratitude deep into your subconscious mind and you will feel amazing. I also concentrate here on helping you let go of the need to blame, instead finding new and fresh ways of looking at everything outside you, whilst giving you the power to control your thoughts from within. This session builds on the work we have done in the first MP3.

This session will quickly take you into a deep state of relaxation using reinforcement techniques previously learned in the earlier recordings. Your understanding of the Law of Gratitude therapy and suggestions will be delivered beautifully to both your conscious and subconscious while you just relax the time away.

Some examples of the Subliminal Suggestions are:

I am filled with gratitude

I am always looking for ways to thank the universe

I am more and more grateful as each day goes by

MP3 3: Understanding the Law of Attraction

Cogni-Fusion 6 Layer Session: This MP3s also deals with Key Issue 5: Lack of Patience.

When you truly understand the Law of Attraction, and start seriously applying it in your life, your whole perspective will shift because you will now start to question everything you have previously thought in the light of your new knowledge. You will start to see small changes in how you perceive everything and everyone around you, and when you start seeing the profound truths in action for yourself, you will be thrilled and want more.

This 6-layer Cogni-Fusion MP3 brings elements of echoes, reverb and bilateral panning in dual audio, creating an ethereal feeling of deep relaxation further enhanced by theta waves.

Your understanding of the Law of Attraction therapy and suggestions will be delivered beautifully to both your conscious and subconscious. Also combining hypnosis, relaxation, positive audible suggestion and Subliminal Suggestions to ensure your understanding of the Law of Attraction and your ability to be patient are driven deeply into your subconscious.

Some examples of the Subliminal Suggestions:

The Law of Attraction is working for me

I attract everything I desire

I am powerful and in the flow

I thank the universe often

MP3 4: Understanding the Law of Abundance

Cogni-Fusion 7 Layer Session: This MP3 also deals purely with the Law of Abundance

The Universal Law of Abundance is an absolute fact and works as well as the Law of Gravity. You do not have to see it to know it is there, and has been since the dawn of time. You just need to believe it, and know that it will work for you. By following the guidelines laid out in this book, and listening to every one of the tracks, you will soon know too that it is a reality that works for you.

This is a 7-layer Cogni-Fusion MP3, combining hypnosis, relaxation, positive audible suggestion and subliminal suggestions. This recording is extremely mellow, with a dominant but quiet layer of Isochronic Tones to take your brain down into a gentle state of deep relaxation. I have overlaid the track with ambient music, making this overall an extremely powerful, complex recording that you will want to play again and again.

Some examples of the Subliminal Suggestions:

The universe is abundant

I am abundant

I attract abundance

The universe wants me to live in joy and happiness

MP3 5: Committing to Your Wealth Creation

Cogni-Fusion 7 Layer Session: This MP3s deals with Key Issues   specific to your Wealth Creation Desires

You are now at the stage where you have eliminated the negative beliefs and limited thinking that previously held you back. You have embraced the Universal Laws and you know that they have already begun working for you. You are now fully ready to embrace and affirm your commitment to your wealth creation – whether that is financial, emotional, spiritual or physical wealth, you now take this incredible opportunity lock this deeply into your subconscious mind.

This incredibly powerful 7-layer Cogni-Fusion recording uses layers of suggestion for relaxation, then moves into therapy, metaphor, and subliminal affirmation and will take you deep into the recesses of your subconscious, enabling you to firmly and fully commit to your long-term wealth creation. This recording utilizes Brainwave Entrainment protocol with binaural beats.

Some examples of the Subliminal Suggestions:

I am fully 100% committed to my wealth creation

I attract money to me and I am attractive to money

I am open to receive wealth in all its forms

Bonus MP3 1: Powerhouse 5 - Specifically for daytime listening

This is a power-packed 3 layered recoding with ALL the suggestions from the 5 core MP3s embedded beneath a focus Brainwave Entrainment track with Isochronic tones in Beta Protocol (which facilitates focus and concentration) and means you can listen to this track during the day whilst you work. I recommend you listen to this regularly once you have gone through the core 5 several times. This will ensure that all of those suggestions are kept fresh and reinforced in your subconscious that you can listen to time and time again whilst you are working, travelling or even doing chores.

Bonus MP3 2: Creative Visualization - Nature Trail

Nature sounds have a way of keeping you in touch with the power of the universe so this is an especially great recording if you do not get much time to spend in nature. As you begin to relax and listen, you will feel as if you are there!

This beautiful 6 layer Cogni-Fusion MP3 has been carefully crafted to enable the complete beginner to learn the simple but vital art of creative visualization. Complex layering over seven tracks of nature sounds takes you on a wondrous journey that has within it the ability to transport you to a completely different world, wherein you can imagine and visualize all your dreams coming true. Not only will this help you hone your visualization skills, it will also attune you to the power of the universe.

Bonus MP3 3: Meditation

Do you often find yourself enjoying a little daydream escapism? This 10 Hz Alpha session mimics the state you get into when you gaze out the window, or zone out from your surroundings for a while and just let your imagination wander. It is a natural thing we all do. This simple 2-layer recording session will help you get into that zone quite easily and is perfect for beginners to meditation. I recommend you use it when you begin your meditation practice.

Graph Refs cited in Chapter Three

http://www.epa.gov/

http://www.lovefoodhatewaste.com/node/2163

http://www.unep.org/

http://www.theglobalmail.org/feature/just-how-fat-are-we/270/

The End... but really, just the beginning for you!

Ok, so that brings us to the end of the book... but your journey has only just begun. Start now, writing down your thoughts, using the questions, and most importantly, listening to those recordings and you will see rapid results. I guarantee it! I hope you will share your journey with me and I look forward to hearing about your progress. You are welcome to email me at any time with your thoughts and questions if you have any. This is just the beginning for you! Believe it!

About the Author

As a qualified Clinical NLP/Hypnotherapist & Personal Development Author, Maria McMahon has helped countless people let go of the negative internal programming that has held them back from living life fully and freely. Her innovative recordings use multi-layering in a unique and inspiring way that brings people results much faster than standard hypnosis recordings, allowing them to quickly overcome all kinds of limiting beliefs, actions and behaviors, to live their lives more fully and more freely.

Maria's Mind Expansion Programs nurture you to dig deep inside yourself to learn about what is really holding you back, and when you do, with the help of her 'Cogni-Fusion' Audios and Program, she promises you will see amazing and fast results in your life.

A lover of travel and international culture, over the last 30 years Maria has lived in Germany, London, Hong Kong, Dubai, Abu Dhabi and Azerbaijan, but she recently moved to Southern Spain to be closer to her family. She is an animal lover, vegetarian and shares her views of the Mediterranean from her apartment with her rescue dogs, Levi from Dubai, and Skye, from Spain.

Maria can be contacted via email or her websites and promises she always replies to her emails personally and has created a special, private email solely for readers of this book.

Email: mailto:mariaprivatemembers@gmail.com

Website: http://www.mariamcmahon.com

Facebook: https://www.facebook.com/mariamcmahoncognifusion/

Final Word from Maria

Dear Reader,

Thank you once again for downloading this book & audios. I am immensely grateful to you!

If you have enjoyed this book and the audios, please consider leaving a review on Amazon, goodreads or your favourite book site, giving your honest feedback. You can comment for example, on:

- What you liked most about the book
- What you liked most about the audios
- What you didn't like about anything
- What was the biggest take-away
- How did this book compare to other books you've read in this category? And by all means cite any books you'd compare this one to.
- Do you think this system offers value for money?
- Did the book cover the content as described?
- What could be improved?
- Any other comments you feel appropriate?

… such feedback not only helps other readers to make informed choices, it also helps authors who continually strive to make their work better for their readers. Reviews are so important for authors and I would be immensely grateful for even a short review and thank you most sincerely.

Maria McMahon

Printed in Great Britain
by Amazon